D0741926

# The Affordable
# Computer

# The Affordable Computer

Microcomputer Applications
in Business and Industry

*Claire Summer*
*Walter A. Levy*

*EDITORS*

## amacom

A Division of American Management Associations

Library of Congress Cataloging in Publication Data

Main entry on the title:

The Affordable computer.

   Includes index.
   1.  Business--Data processing--Addresses, essays,
lectures.  2.  Miniature computers--Addresses, essays,
lectures.  I.  Summer, Claire.  II. Levy, Walter A.
HF5548.2.A44     001.6'4'024658     78-23754
ISBN 0-8144-5493-3

# Contents

**6** Microcomputers Provide Accounting Benefits to
   Small Businesses                                                                78

A Beer and Wine Wholesaler / An Auto Parts
Distributor / A Clothing Manufacturer / A Door
and Window Manufacturer / A Hospital Supplier /
A Lumber Distributor / A House-Plant Distributor /
An Accounting Firm / A Microcomputer Supplier for
Medical Offices / A Retail Supplies Manufacturer /
An Air Freight Company / An Air Pollution Filtration
Manufacturer / A Farming Cooperative / A County
Government / A City Government / A Beer Distribu-
tor / A Marine Supplier / An Auto Parts Manufacturer

**7** Microcomputers Help Small Businesses Manage
   and Produce Revenues                                                         113

A Real Estate Investment Firm / A Transport
Service / An Architectural Planning Company / A
Radio Station / A Mortgage Company / A Trucking
Company / A Kitchen Accessories Supplier / A
Building Materials Outlet / An Auto Parts Supplier /
A Seafood Importer / A Brokerage Firm /
A Miniconglomerate / A Broadcasting Company /
A Travel Firm / A Hotel Operator / A Real Estate
Agency / A Food Supplier / A Textile Rental
Company / A Commodities Trading Center / An
Insurance Company

# Introduction
# to Minicomputers

TWENTY years ago, a high school boy would save up his earnings from delivering newspapers and buy a bicycle. Today, for the same money, he can walk into a local store and buy a computer.

Until recently, computers were multimillion-dollar tools of only the largest organizations. Now, thanks to a galloping technology, computers suitable for business use can be bought for less than the price of a delivery truck. For under $10,000, any business can think of having its own microcomputer.

Until the advent of these incredibly low-cost systems, computers were built and sold only by large national companies such as IBM and Univac. Now microcomputers are being built and sold directly to consumers and many businesses by retail stores and dealers. The corner candy store has been remodeled into the corner computer store.

For the small business, these new computers may offer a real bargain. If you can buy a basic system for less than $10,000 that will automate your accounts receivable or inventory control, you won't need much in the way of reduced bad receivables or inventory turnover to justify the purchase. A

$10,000 computer pays for itself in one year if it eliminates just one clerical job.

The great thing about computers is that they "can do." They'll do just about anything if you program them properly. But learning to program them has cost large companies countless millions. Small companies can't afford the same mistakes. Moreover, computers can (and do) break down, and businesses lose money waiting for the repair service. The small business with a $10,000 computer isn't likely to get the same service as the million-dollar IBM installation. The user of a microcomputer must rely on a local supplier to service the system and to make new equipment features and programs available. Many companies went into the computer business and disappeared, leaving a trail of frustrated customers. IBM is here to stay, but will the corner computer store be here tomorrow?

The opportunity to get inexpensive computer power is very exciting, but the small business must be careful. The microcomputer is very new, and there are a lot of questions to answer. First, exactly what do microcomputers do? How much of what you read about them is true? What do they really cost? What benefits can they provide to the small business? What kind of trouble might you have purchasing and installing these new computers, and how can you protect yourself? Finally, how do you get started?

## What Is a Microcomputer?

A microcomputer is a simple, lightweight, inexpensive computer system. But it is not lightweight when it comes to producing results. Today's microcomputer has as much processing power as yesterday's multimillion-dollar giant. Thanks to the miracle of the microprocessor chip—the postage-stamp-size integrated circuit that has replaced rooms full of equipment—practical amounts of computing power are now within nearly everyone's reach.

In its business applications, a computer maintains accounting records, calculates invoices, posts receivables, prepares the payroll, and keeps track of inventory levels. Large computers have been providing these services for years at a price beyond the reach of most businesses. Microcomputers can provide the same services now, and at a price nearly all businesses can afford.

In addition to being smaller and far less costly than the older and larger systems, microcomputers are simpler to program, operate, and maintain. Because of their physical simplicity, they are less likely to break down than large systems, and repairs are easier to make. The user of a large computer system must maintain a staff of experts at programming and operation. In contrast, the small business owner can train a secretary or bookkeeper to operate a microcomputer and have a local college student come in once in a while to write special programs. In short, the basic problems of running a computer have not changed, but things have become much simpler and more manageable with microcomputers.

Today's microcomputer systems are built of four basic components: the file storage unit, processor, keyboard–video display work station, and printer.

### *File Storage Unit*

Most business accounting problems call for the computer to hold in storage a complete functional file such as accounts receivable or accounts payable. Each day, data on business transactions are entered into the machine. The computer processes the transactions against the entire file, updates each active account, and produces invoices, trial balances, paychecks, and any reports required.

In a microcomputer, these files are magnetically recorded on a rotating plastic disk (called "floppy" because it is flexible). Data can be read from or written to the disk via a movable magnetic head, so the disk resembles a phonograph record with a tape head rather than a needle as the pickup.

A typical disk holds roughly 250,000 characters of information (which might correspond to 500 stock records, each having up to 500 characters of information). The computer can get at any record stored on disk in less than one second. Disks can be interchanged like phonograph records, so there is no real limit to the size or variety of files that can be handled by a microcomputer.

### Processor

All program functions of the microcomputer are carried out in the processor. The programs that the processor executes are normally stored in the processor's "main memory." Programs not always required in main memory are stored on a disk. Today's microcomputers have a main-memory capacity of up to 64,000 characters. This is enough to hold programs of sufficient power and flexibility to meet the accounting needs of most businesses. Since additional programs can be stored on disk and brought into main memory on demand, there is no real limit to the number or variety of program functions of the microcomputer. A single computer system can be used for accounts receivable one day, inventory control the next, and payroll the next, simply by loading the appropriate programs and files into the machine for each application.

### Keyboard–Video Display Work Station

In any accounting system, the user must enter data into the computer for such purposes as (1) adding records to files or changing record contents, (2) recording daily business transactions such as cash receipts and order bookings, and (3) obtaining information such as stock availability or customer account status from files stored in the computer. Microcomputer systems commonly include a data-entry and quick-response work station that combines a keyboard and video display.

The operator enters information through the keyboard,

and the computer presents this information on the video display for confirmation. In some systems the computer assists in the correct entry of data by prompting the operator with queries on the video display. Responses to inquiries from the operator can also be presented through the video display. If the amount of information is too great or a permanent record of the data is required, a printer must be used.

The combination keyboard–video display work station is quite satisfactory for daily business operations. However, it is not efficient for entering large amounts of data, as when initially loading a large file. In this case, the user can have a service bureau card-punch the file and load the disk cartridges at a large computer data center.

### *Printer*

Every business accounting function requires printed documents such as invoices, paychecks, and general ledger trial balances. A printer capable of producing these documents is an essential element of a microcomputer business system. Many inexpensive printers are being marketed with microcomputers. Some of these are suitable only for scientific, hobbyist, or industrial applications. Of the printers now being marketed with microcomputers, only the more expensive ones have the format, print quality, printing speed, and reliability that the general business accounting system needs.

The four components are very compact. A complete working system can fit on top of an office desk and operate in any room that is comfortable and temperate. Figures 1 and 2 illustrate typical microcomputer systems. Figure 1 shows a complete system being used by its owner, a small plumbing contractor. The three cabinets to the left front of the operator contain the processor and its main memory, the keyboard–video display work station, and provisions for two disk cartridge drives. To the operator's right front stands the keyboard printer. Figure 2 gives a view of another manufacturer's product in which all functions except the printer are combined into one housing.

**Figure 1.**

Photograph reproduced courtesy of Pertec Computer Corporation, Los Angeles, California.

**Figure 2.**

Photograph reproduced courtesy of IMSAI Manufacturing Corporation, San Leandro, California.

## A Few Facts about Programs

Microcomputers, like their costly predecessors, require well-designed and thoroughly tested programs if they are to supply small businesses with useful and trouble-free accounting services. There are two basic classes of programs that a small business will encounter in the course of acquiring and/or developing an accounting system.

### System Programs

System programs control the fundamental computer operations that underlie almost every application, whether it is accounts receivable, payroll, or sales analysis. Programs that translate user-oriented programming language into a form directly usable by the computer are also called system programs. These basic programs are generally manufacturer-furnished with the equipment and are usually trouble-free and predictable in behavior. But they are only a foundation for the application programs, which do the actual work.

### Application Programs

Application programs perform useful business services such as posting or aging accounts receivable and calculating payroll. These programs are usually custom-written to the user's specifications. Customized application programs are costly and rarely trouble-free. They are constantly subject to change in response to changing business needs.

Software companies have developed standardized programs for common business applications and offer them at prices far below the cost of custom-written programs. Many of these software products are quite reliable and powerful and offer a genuine bargain to users who are willing to accept the standardized features and adapt their operations accordingly.

Like custom-written programs, standardized programs are subject to change if the needs of the business change. A new tax law or a new discount policy may require modification of even the best and most reliable of programs. When the need for change arises, standardized programs have both advantages and disadvantages compared with custom programs. If the change is one that affects most businesses, like a new tax law, the supplier of the standard program will probably make the necessary modifications, test them thoroughly, and provide all users with an inexpensive and reliable set of new features. If the change is one that only a particular business requires, the user may experience great difficulty and expense in requesting the supplier to "custom-alter" the standardized program.

Custom application programs can generally be afforded only by large corporations. They are out of the question for the small business contemplating a $10,000 computer. For most small business users, standardized software packages will become a way of life.

### How Much Does a Microcomputer Cost?

The console illustrated in Figure 2 contains the processor with its memory, two disk drives, and the keyboard–video display unit, all integrated into a single housing. This unit, with 32,000 characters of main memory, sells for about $6,000. With the full-size, 64,000 characters of memory, the console costs about $7,000. Several printers available for microcomputers will produce output of acceptable quality for business use. They range in price from $2,000 to $3,000, depending on speed, ruggedness, and print quality.

Thus the system illustrated in Figure 2 might cost between $8,000 and $10,000 at today's prices. However, these figures cover only the bare equipment itself and perhaps some manufacturer-furnished system programs. The buyer also has to consider the costs of maintenance and of application programs. Maintenance-price quotes are not easily available, but dealers generally estimate maintenance costs at $1,500 per year, or $125 per month for such a system.

With only one known exception, none of the manufacturers of microcomputers is as yet offering generalized business application programs. The one company that has taken this step has established a national software distribution group and has announced a line of common business applications. A license to use each application can be purchased for about $1,100, and all can be integrated:

- General ledger
- Accounts receivable
- Accounts payable
- Inventory control

For the quoted price, the user gets a license to use the program on a single computer, a copy of the program, instructions on its installation and use, and some training from the manufacturer's local dealer. These packages are very attractive if they can give the user satisfactory service without customization. (The company strongly discourages users from thinking about customization.)

Many small software companies and dealers in small computers have developed low-cost business application programs and are marketing them through word of mouth or mail-order advertising. Again, users get the program, some instructional material, and a "hearty handshake." They are really on their own. But the software is cheap.

Most users of microcomputer business systems have either developed the application programs themselves or purchased the entire system (equipment and applications) through a turnkey supplier. The supplier puts a fixed price on the complete system, generally in the range of two to three times the equipment cost, and contracts to deliver a working end product. Although this approach theoretically costs the user more than buying the equipment directly from the manufacturer, purchasing a low-cost software package, and trying to put the two together, it is almost the only way to get a working system without becoming a computer expert in the process. Realistically, in today's market a turnkey-installed general accounting system, based on about $10,000 worth of equipment, is going to cost from $20,000 to $25,000. It's still a bargain, however, if it solves the user's problems.

Are today's prices "high"? Should you go ahead now and feel foolish next year because prices have dropped? The best answer is probably not. It is doubtful if the basic equipment cost will drop below $8,000 in the foreseeable future. The benefits of microprocessor technology are already fully reflected in the low cost of the computer, and the printer, which is the key element for business application, is unlikely to get much cheaper. Software prices are also likely to remain the same, since most suppliers are already "investing in the future" by setting prices low in the expectation of volume sales. If anything, software prices will rise as marginal suppliers leave the market. If a system does not seem like a "good buy" for your business at today's prices, price reductions in the near future are not going to change your decision.

## What Are the Benefits to a Small Business?

Microcomputers are well suited to the general accounting and management needs of most small businesses. Nearly all businesses need the following more or less standard accounting services and recordkeeping functions:

- General ledger
- Accounts receivable
- Accounts payable
- Payroll and personnel records
- Order processing and invoicing
- Inventory control and purchases
- Sales analysis
- Budgeting and planning

Many businesses also require such control functions as:

- Labor distribution and cost accounting
- Advertising and mailing lists
- Cash flow projections and check reconciliation

Governments and school districts may require such special functions as:

- Tax assessment and billing
- Student records and report cards
- Classroom scheduling

The microcomputer can perform any or all of these functions, plus countless other special applications, subject to the following conditions:

- The user can get application programs that are well designed, thoroughly tested, and reasonably priced.
- The user's physical workload is within the capacity of the equipment. (Even if programs were available, a 10,000-employee payroll could not be processed on a microcomputer; however, 100 employees could be easily handled in a day.)
- The equipment can handle the daily workload with a minimum of maintenance, and downtime for repairs will not hamper the user's operations. (Heavy-duty computer printers can run for hours at a time, producing millions of lines of print without breaking down. Less costly, lighter-duty microcomputer printers cannot.)

The computer system, if properly designed and tested, will improve the user's operations in a number of ways. The system will enable the user to eliminate tedious yet costly clerical tasks, to keep more accurate records of the state of the business, and to make better decisions. In addition, businesses can expect automation of each traditional accounting function to yield certain types of benefits. For example:

- Automating inventory management should reduce inventories relative to volume and produce a better return on capital.
- Automating receivables should reduce delinquencies, pinpoint bad credit risks before they get out of hand,

speed up payments from good customers, and calculate and verify fast payment discounts.

- Automating purchasing and payables should improve cash flow through careful scheduling of deliveries and payments and reduce costs for materials and shipping through consolidation of purchases and deliveries.
- Automating order processing and billing should accelerate inventory turnover, improve sales through prompt and accurate delivery to customers, and speed up cash flow through prompt and accurate billing.

Large businesses, using larger computers, have generally experienced these benefits. There is every reason to expect smaller businesses to have the same results with microcomputers.

## Where to Buy a Microcomputer System

Microcomputers are available from local computer stores and turnkey system contractors. It sounds simple, but it's really revolutionary. The multimillion-dollar computer industry is sedate by comparison. About ten companies in this country manufacture and sell large computers (such as IBM and Univac) and minicomputers (such as Digital Equipment Corp. and Data General Corp.) These companies market a line of products nationally through company-owned offices. Users get the same product at the same price whether they buy it in Albuquerque, New Mexico, or Brooklyn, New York. If the local service people cannot solve a problem, the company will fly in help from the home office. Application software has always been a local problem. Some buyers of large computers develop their own applications; others contract (usually locally) with a software supplier or purchase a software product.

With a microcomputer, the user is dealing almost exclusively with a local supplier. Currently about ten companies manufacture microcomputers, but none of them sell directly to end users. They all reach the public through independent dealers. In addition, a number of small companies manufacture or distribute components for microcomputers.

Unlike the older and larger computers, microcomputer systems can be assembled from commonly available and inexpensive components. The microcomputer market is a hobbyist's paradise, and literally hundreds of companies, either computer stores or turnkey system contractors, are *assembling* their own computers and selling them to you.

Do you really want to buy a computer that was assembled by a local dealer? What happens if it fails? Will the computer store know how to fix it and be willing to fix it for a reasonable price? If you buy the system outright and the store cannot maintain it at a reasonable price, what recourse do you have? Will the store still be in business in a year or two? You can't sue a business that isn't there.

Let's not be alarmist. It is unfair to exaggerate the negative possibilities. Microcomputers are extremely simple and inherently reliable. Furthermore, the microcomputer industry has already achieved an excellent level of standardization of components. These machines are basically simpler than stereo equipment or videotape recorders—and they are easier to assemble and repair. In all probability, any microcomputer store with qualified service personnel will be able to repair a system assembled by another store and furnish new features or add-on memory at a reasonable price.

In the long run, the computer stores and small turnkey system contractors are going to provide small businesses with a valuable product. At present, small suppliers are still learning how to support the business community, and buyers have to watch out for a few problems. Many computer stores, for example, deal largely with hobbyists: young, technically sophisticated customers who buy pieces of a computer to put together at home and who do not require support or maintenance.

Businesses, however, need to have their problems solved and equipment serviced at the touch of a telephone. Most computer stores are not yet set up to supply complete integrated systems and maintain them. The printer, while not important to a hobbyist, is a critical part of a business system. It is also far more complex, trouble-prone, and difficult to fix than all the other microcomputer components put together. Very few if any small suppliers can afford to keep the parts and trained personnel to maintain these printers. Of seven computer stores recently interviewed in the greater New York area, all of which sold systems to small businesses, only one was willing to even quote maintenance on the printer, let alone claim it would have the parts and personnel to do the work.

Buyers must be even more cautious when considering software. The safest approach, at present, is to contract with a turnkey supplier for a complete system that meets your functional specifications. You will have one supplier, responsible for integrating all the equipment and programs and providing a working end product. Every successful microcomputer installation reported in this book is of that type.

But the turnkey approach is not perfect. In nearly every case, the price of a turnkey system is based on the supplier's ability to use the same basic programs on many installations, making limited changes to satisfy the individual requirements of each customer. Otherwise, suppliers would have to charge $100,000 for a custom system—rather than $20,000, which is about what the user will pay. The problem with this approach is that no two sets of programs installed by a supplier are identical, and when you request some changes, you may be asking for a customized system at a much higher price.

By contrast, a well-developed generalized software product is supported throughout its marketplace by a single supplier. If you can find one for your particular application, you will have a very powerful and flexible product that will probably cost less than the software supplied with a turnkey installation. Hundreds of small companies are offering software products for microcomputers at anywhere from $9.95 to $2,000. They advertise in trade journals and sell through computer stores. However, microprocessor business application software is still a relatively new and unproven field. Microcomputer business applications have to perform functions comparable to programs that run on larger computers. Good general ledger software products for large IBM computers, for instance, sell for $20,000 to $30,000 per installation and require a professional staff to install. Only time will tell whether the software industry can successfully market simpler programs of similar quality for microcomputers—at a fraction of the cost.

## Getting Started

The successful buyer is a well-educated buyer. Begin by learning as much as you can about microcomputer systems. You would be wise not to program your own system at first, but you should understand enough about the underlying technology, hardware, and software to make intelligent and informed decisions.

Go to a computer store and let the clerks tell you what they can. Pick up some good books on data processing management. Such books are primarily addressed to the large computer centers of big corporations, but they present sound ideas on managing a computer operation that apply to any installation.

Try to formulate a definite idea of what you want to accomplish with *your* computer system. When you begin to talk to suppliers (by the way, be sure you get at least two competitive bids), you will benefit from their ideas and expertise. But be sure the system you buy is one that you want, not one that you are sold. The more thoroughly you can define what you want and describe it in technical terms, the easier it will be to obtain competitive bids and get what you need. Don't expect the suppliers to second-guess you. If you do not know how big your files are or how many orders per month you process, find out before you begin shopping for a system.

Cultivate two or more qualified suppliers. Take your time,

get to know them, talk with some satisfied customers, and find out if the suppliers are really comfortable with business data processing installations. Give them a chance to explain the benefits of using their software products. After all, if a supplier has something you could use without difficulty, it might be better to adapt your methods a little than to rigidly insist on your initial requirements.

If you decide to proceed, write out the simplest and clearest statement of what you need, discuss it with each bidder, and ask for proposals that respond both technically and from a contractual or business viewpoint. Be prepared to commit yourself to working closely with the chosen supplier throughout the planning, development, and installation of the system. Unless you work hand in glove with a supplier, you are going to have trouble. You should certainly be businesslike and hold your supplier accountable for performance. But the supplier is not an adversary or someone who must deliver goods regardless of what you do. No supplier has ever successfully installed a computer system without the wholehearted cooperation of the user.

Thoroughness and attention to detail are essential throughout the installation. The introduction of a computer will affect every aspect of your business. New forms and procedures will be required. Things that might not have mattered before, like the exact spelling of a customer's name, will suddenly become important. You must be prepared to train your staff and, more important, to make sure that everyone accepts the new way of operation. Do not try to convert your operations during a busy season or when your business is going through a significant change, such as opening a new plant or changing a key supplier. One thing at a time is enough.

One last word of caution. Even under the best of conditions, computer installations do not proceed smoothly. Delays must be anticipated. Do not cut the cord with the past. Keep your old systems and methods in place. If possible, test the new system against the old. Even after you install the new system, make sure you will be able to fall back on your old methods, if necessary, for at least a few months after conversion. Run quickly from anyone who tells you otherwise.

## Evaluating the Benefits After Installation

An investment of $20,000 is a big step for the small business. In theory, you estimated where you would get the benefits before buying a system, and now that the computer is installed and running smoothly you should be able to observe if you were right. Right? Not necessarily.

You may have estimated that a clerical position could be eliminated after the system was operating. If you laid off the clerk, fine. But maybe you decided to give the clerk other duties. You may have estimated that automating your receivables would cut bad debt losses by 5 percent. Now that the computer is working, you figure you should be able to compare this year's bad debt losses with last year's. But no two years are alike. Maybe this year your customers happen to be in better shape and are paying their bills.

Rarely do first-time computer users merely plug the system into their business operations without making substantial changes. It's not easy to make a before-and-after comparison with everything unchanged except for the computer. The real test is to watch your business carefully to see, on a day-to-day basis, if things really are getting better. There is no substitute for this kind of close observation both during and after the computer installation.

There is no reason why you cannot take advantage of a powerful and inexpensive microcomputer system to make your business more competitive, more profitable, and easier to run. The experiences reported in the remainder of this book will help you decide if a microcomputer business system will work for you. The articles should give you an idea of the costs and capacity of different types of microcomputers, the variety of application programs available, and the range of benefits these systems provide.

The intent of this book is to help you understand the

power of microcomputers and how they can be used successfully in the daily management of your business. This is not a
book about computer theory or how to assemble and program
your own machine. It is a book about the realities of the
microcomputer market today: who is selling these systems,
who has bought them and used them successfully in small
business operations, and, most important, how careful buyers
of microcomputer systems have gotten their money's worth.

# 1   CARL WARREN

# Basic Principles of Automated Accounting

*Any accounting system, whether manual or automated, must follow certain principles. The small business office incorporates these principles in its daily operations as a matter of course. Rarely are accounting principles studied systematically; common sense and close working relationships within the office generally determine what accounting procedures to use.*

*When the small business decides to automate its accounting functions, a new viewpoint must be adopted. Before a computer can be introduced to the office, all existing procedures must be carefully reviewed and documented. The computerized accounting system may work differently from existing manual methods; and if the business is to take advantage of all the features of the computer system, it may have to change its methods. Regardless of the final form of the new accounting system, its introduction requires a systematic review of the flow of financial and operational data within*

CARL WARREN is Senior Editor, *Interface Age Magazine.* This chapter is a selection from his book *From the Counter to the Bottom Line.* Portland, Ore.: Dilithium Press, 1978. It is reprinted with permission.

the business. For many small businesses, this review may provide a unique opportunity—after years of successful but informally managed operations—to study accounting principles as an organized body of knowledge.

The following article presents a systems-oriented view of the general accounting functions required by most small businesses. It was written by a computer expert who is knowledgeable in accounting principles and shows the systematic process-flow viewpoint common to the computer field. An understanding of this viewpoint is essential for any small business that contemplates purchasing its own computer system. Vendors of accounting programs or turnkey system suppliers tend to think along these lines, describe their offerings accordingly, and try to persuade users to think the same way.

## The Basics of an Accounting Package

THE problem of discussing automated business systems is that it is sometimes difficult to relate the concept to real-life situations. This is sometimes the result of not having sufficient information with which to work. Therefore, it becomes important to start at the beginning and proceed from that point.

The first question that one might ask is: "What is automated accounting?" A simple answer is that it is a method of using the power of the computer to handle inventory, billing, accounts receivable, accounts payable, and payroll. Automated business systems also provide for a logical flow of bookkeeping and of updating records.

Figure 1 is an example of the general makeup and flow of an automated system. However, in order to fully understand the concept of an automated system, some terms must be defined.

Accounting is the measurement of business activity. In other words, all functions that make up a business environment are tracked. An accounting package is a collection of subsystems that are designed to provide meaningful mea-

**Figure 1.**

GENERAL LEDGER

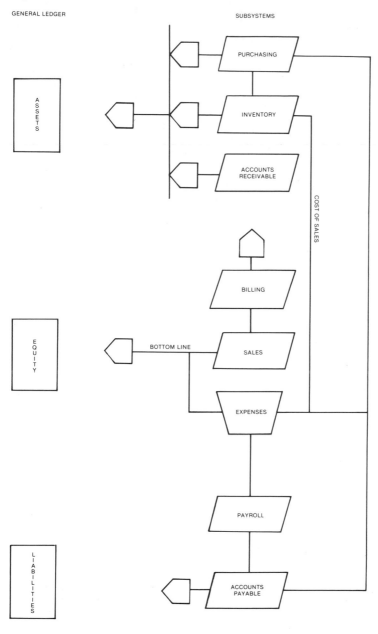

surement of each area of a general business activity. An accounting package generally contains the following subsystems:

- Inventory control
- Accounts receivable and billing
- Accounts payable
- General ledger

A subsystem, in automated accounting, represents a detailed list with a total that stands alone. The subsystem is in fact a stand-alone system, created to be interactive with other subsystems.

The automated accounting package is both a horizontal and vertical system. Each of the major subsystems supplies data to the general ledger, while at the same time affecting each other. For example, the *inventory control* subsystem horizontally affects the assets picture of the general ledger but at the same time affects the accounts payable subsystem. This in turn generates figures for the general ledger, under liabilities and equity, and of course produces the bottom line or profit/ loss picture. An accounting package is interactive, each part depending upon the other.

Now it becomes important to redefine automated accounting. Automated accounting, or a computerized business system, is a collection of several small subsystems, designated by task, working in such a manner to provide stand-alone and integrated totals representing business activity.

Referring again to Figure 1, let's look at the makeup of each of the subsystems as separate entities, and how they interact. The first subsystem is *inventory control*. This system is really made up of two smaller systems; purchasing and inventory. Together they make up the *inventory control* package. From Figure 1 it is seen that inventory must be purchased, thus creating expenses that can be grouped under the heading of the cost of doing business. At the same time, the assumption is made that if you are buying inventory, you plan to sell. Consequently, this moves you into the *accounts receivable/billing* package.

The *accounts receivable/billing* package is a direct result of sales. Sales create a billing situation, which generates *accounts receivable*. The inventory and accounts receivable grouped together become a major portion of current assets. When the inventory is purchased and received, assets are acquired, and you also owe the supplier. You now have *accounts payable*.

Together, expenses, borrowing, and the purchase of assets create liabilities, which is another major area of the general ledger. When the amount of revenue coming in versus the amount of expenses going out is calculated, the bottom line is created, which becomes part of the equity of the business, either plus or minus.

Accounting systems, whether they are manual or automated, must be understood in order to receive the greatest benefit. Up to this point, I have discussed basically what an accounting package is. Now it is important to look at the total system flow of an automated system.

To fully understand the makeup of the accounting package, look at the interactive block diagram shown in Figure 2. You will notice that the diagram shows the general ledger in the center with the four major subsystems *inventory control, accounts receivable/billing, accounts payable* and *payroll* surrounding it. Each subsystem generates specific data that can, as I said before, be used alone and then handed off to the general ledger package. Each of the blocks making up the subsystems and general ledger represent a specific function to be performed within the entire package. Admittedly, this is a simplification of an automated accounting package, but it does offer the basic design.

## A Peek at Inventory Control

The *inventory control* package is important because it gives you better control over what you sell. By having this control

**Figure 2.**

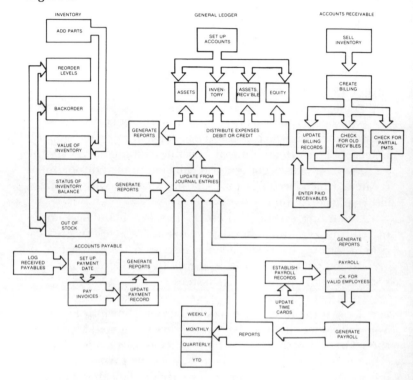

you will be able to regulate the other portions of your business.

The *inventory control* package allows you statusing capability of inventory balances. What does that mean? For each item that your business handles you can, at a glance, determine the current level of each item and what items you have in inventory at any given time. For example, suppose you are the owner of a small paint store carrying 20 different colors of paint. It is important for you to know exactly how many gallons, quarts, and pints you have on hand in each color. More important, you probably would like to know which colors are selling the best and which ones are not: a ranking of fast to slow movers. An inventory control package gives you this ability.

Another important item to know about, when controlling your inventory, is to determine which items bring you the greatest profit based on costs, overhead, etc. By using the information from the inventory balances, and the fast to slow ranking, a decision on what you should carry the greatest inventory level on can be made.

By maintaining proper inventory balances, capital investment and inventory taxes can be reduced. An inventory package is set up in such a way to monitor the minimum number of stock quantities needed and flag items below that point. Also, it indicates which items are at maximum levels. Items that are out of stock are flagged and monitored so that they are not forgotten if backordered from a supplier. Backordered parts are monitored so that a tight rein can be kept on the supplier.

To review what the inventory control package can do for a small business:

- Give the status of inventory balances.
- Differentiate fast movers from slow movers.
- Determine high-profit items from low-profit items.
- Help reduce stock levels by keeping track of minimum/maximum order points.
- Flag out-of-stock items and keep track of backordered items.

But that's not all an *inventory control* package does. If manual, it helps the bookkeeper or inventory control clerk generate reports. On an automated system, reports are generated by the computer, giving a list of the inventory in order of total value or by item number.

To get an idea of what should happen when controlling inventory, look at the flow chart in Figure 3. From the chart, you can see that stock is purchased to sell. In some cases, the items are not readily available from the supplier and must be

**Figure 3.**

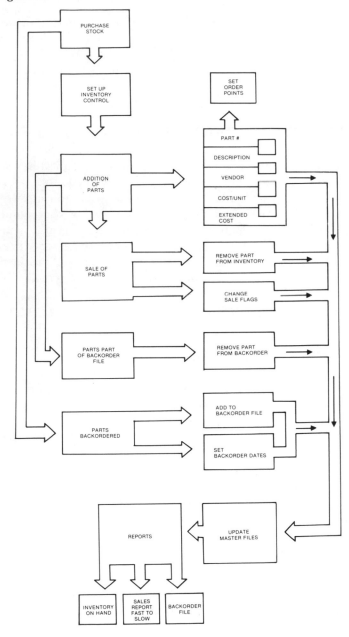

backordered; more on this later. Once the stock is purchased, some method of control must be set up. This is a way of determining total inventory on hand, value of the inventory, out-of-stock items, items that are below or at reorder points, and backordered items. All these areas of inventory become extremely important when trying to manage the day-to-day operation of a small business.

When an item is added, certain information must be kept regarding the actual item. Also, depending upon past sales history or plain old gut feeling, reorder points must be indicated.

Probably one of the most important features of a viable inventory control package is that of keeping track of what is and is not selling and how fast. This information allows you to make intelligent determinations of what items to keep and what to drop.

The purpose of inventory control is to give the businessman complete and absolute control of the whole inventory. Having this information allows him to develop reports and make comparisons of fast to slow movers. By maintaining the proper inventory records, the exact levels of all the items and, more important, the exact cost of the inventory, are known at a glance. From this type of information, projections and sound business decisions can be made.

Backordered items are the oddballs and must be treated completely different from actual on-hand items. Now, referring again to Figure 3, you can see that the actual items received are added to the on-hand items, but backordered items are added to a new record called the backorder file, which contains all the information as in the on-hand file but with dates indicating when the item was ordered and when to expect it. Also, within this file are provisions to indicate that the backordered item is being "held" for a customer. These "held" items are flagged so they are not carried in the general inventory.

Sounds simple, doesn't it? Actually, inventory control is relatively easy depending on your type of business, inventory, and sales profile.

## The User and System Benefits

Who would want a small system accounting package? It is the businessman who is having trouble keeping track of inventory and determining what items are losers and what are gainers. Also, the businessman who is spending extra time in his business after hours bringing his books up to date to analyze daily transactions.

Basically, the user of a small business system is anyone who has decided that his bookkeeping is time-consuming enough to require automation. The following guidelines should be used when determining whether or not you are in need of automation:

- Inventory is large, or varied.
- Receivables consist of both over-the-counter cash and billing.
- Payables are frequent enough to invite automation.
- The general bookkeeping is difficult to handle within normal hours.
- Payroll is time-consuming and manually calculated.

After reviewing your situation you find that you have all five problems or even one, and that the cost of a system does not overshadow the amount of time it saves and the additional effectiveness of evaluating and managing your business; then it is a good idea to automate.

The worst thing that you, the small business owner, can do is to purchase a computer and the necessary software packages thinking it will automatically solve your problems. *It will not.* It will, however, help you pinpoint the areas that need to be watched and help in the management of these problems.

A microcomputer system is needed because it provides the small business with the benefits of a computerized accounting system normally affordable only to large companies. The small computer allows the use of many of the high-level business techniques that normally only much larger businesses use for handling the day-to-day business.

Let's look at exactly what the benefits are: First, by using an automated system you will be able to process information in time enough to make needed projections and make plans that are necessary to the well-being of your business. The next ability a small system gives you is the ease of automated billing. Billing is usually one of the more tiresome items and takes a great deal of time by creating the bill, then booking the receivables and hand-aging them. The automated system is designed to provide a data base for billing, calculating dates for receivable aging, and basically reducing the workload. The next item is to update the receivables ledger and keep track of these necessary items. All of this is done by the computer with speed and accuracy.

Another important aspect of the automated system is that it provides for ease in preparing your financial statements. Also, the statement can be formatted in any row-column structure that fits your specific needs. To review, the benefits of an automated system are:

- Ability to plan
- Automated billing/accounts receivable
- Automated accounts receivable ledger
- Automated payroll
- Speed and accuracy
- Ease in preparation of financial statements

There is still another major benefit that is obtained from using the automated system, and that is it will help to minimize small business failures. Many small businesses fail due to the lack of understanding what is happening, why it's happening, and the lack of sufficient information to analyze it and prevent it. This is not to say that the computer is going to analyze volumes of data for you and make the necessary decisions to keep you in business; nor will it create some wonderful idea that will save an already dying company. Remember, only you can do the decision making, the machine won't; but it will provide you with the information you need.

The information that is available from an automated accounting system gives you the opportunity to measure the performance of your company based on whatever factors you feel are important. By watching cash flow trends and inventory trends and making wise decisions based on this information, you can affect the profit margin of your company.

What I want to make clear is that the computer is not a savior; it is a tool and must be viewed from that aspect. If the computer makes more work for you, it is not valuable. If it causes you a major cash flow problem, it isn't needed at this point. The point is that an automated system is only as good as the user wishes it to be.

# 2    WALTER A. LEVY

# CLAUDIUS:
# A Microcomputer Order Processing System

*This chapter, which was written especially for this volume, describes an integrated system for order processing, inventory control, and general accounting developed and marketed on a turnkey basis by Coopers & Lybrand, one of the world's largest accounting firms. The design of the system reflects the process-flow viewpoint (described by Carl Warren in Chapter 1) and the better-quality features that an experienced developer can provide.*

## Introduction

IN late 1976 the United Kingdom branch of Coopers & Lybrand (C&L) decided to offer its clients a microprocessor-based business data processing system.* Many small and medium-size distributors and manufacturers need good order processing and inventory control systems, but few can afford IBM or comparably priced computers. Computer cost justification is more difficult in the United Kingdom than in the United States, since computers cost more in the United Kingdom and salaries are lower.

Coopers & Lybrand wanted to lower the cost of a computer system as much as possible while providing reliable and productive processing services. The firm decided that this goal could be achieved by using an inexpensive microprocessor system and developing simple, standardized application programs whose costs could be spread among several users.

Coopers & Lybrand accordingly undertook to develop a set of programs, titled CLAUDIUS,* to provide the business management system. The computer that C&L selected for the initial development is the Microfile, manufactured by Data Terminals and Communications in the United States. DTC is one of several companies in the San Francisco area that have adapted the microprocessor chip to their own model computer. DTC is primarily a manufacturer of computer terminals and generally markets the Microfile as an "intelligent terminal." However, a computer it is. The first CLAUDIUS installation will be in the United Kingdom Ministry of Health, where the system will be used to manage an inventory of laboratory supplies dispensed to many different organizations.

A noteworthy feature of CLAUDIUS is the strong attention given to security and good accounting controls. The design of the system provides ample checks and balances to minimize the chance of data entry or processing errors. To the small business that can afford only an economy system, this design

* The microprocessor system is presently being marketed only in the United Kingdom.
* Officially "Coopers & Lybrand Accounting Distributive System," but unofficially named after the Roman emperor who, according to the British Broadcasting Company (BBC), was a good manager.

feature is of considerable importance. Building good accounting controls into the programs is not a luxury if the developer has the know-how and the buyer insists on their presence in the system.

## Objectives of CLAUDIUS

The CLAUDIUS business management system is specifically designed for small and medium-size wholesalers and dealers and for larger businesses with multiple-store locations. Although designed for the distribution industry, the system can also be used in manufacturing and nontrading organizations to assist in stores control, general accounting, order processing, and inventory analysis. CLAUDIUS consists of a series of related computer programs that provide facilities for processing customer orders, maintaining stock records and customer and supplier accounts, and producing sales statistics and financial reports. CLAUDIUS aims to:

- Improve customer service through faster handling of sales orders, faster assembly of orders, and better stock availability.
- Improve stock management by highlighting low or excessive stock positions, recommending reorder quantities, and providing regular reports on stock turnover and valuation.
- Improve margins by regular reviews of sales prices, more accurate pricing and control of stock loss, and better use of staff and space.
- Improve cash flow by regular billing, routine follow-up on overdue accounts, and reduction of stock investment.
- Improve productivity by avoiding copying and multiple handling of source documents through the automatic updating of all associated data from a single input transaction.

**Equipment Used**

CLAUDIUS operates on a desk-top Microfile computer system consisting of a computer processor with 40,000 bytes of main memory; disk drives that provide up to 600,000 characters of data storage; a visual display unit consisting of a keyboard and a display screen; and a printer operating at 30 characters per second (cps). Two additional disk drives may be added to the system, and a choice of printers operating at up to 300 lines per minute (lpm) may replace the 30 cps printer.

**System Capacity**

CLAUDIUS is suitable for small and medium-size organizations. A typical organization might deal with the following volumes:

- 4,000 to 8,000 product lines
- 1,000 to 2,000 customers
- 200 general ledger accounts
- 500 suppliers
- 250 to 500 transactions per day (depending on their complexity)

These volumes are intended as guidelines to the system's capability. Individual applications vary widely, and the system has considerable flexibility; volumes are limited only by the total disk capacity of the computer hardware and the specific CLAUDIUS application modules and options required.

**CLAUDIUS in Operation**

In operation, orders from customers or salesmen for stock items are entered into the system via a keyboard in response to prompts from the computer. The orders are automatically priced and totaled, and a stock file is updated with the sales. The stock file contains information such as line number, product description, unit price, number in pack, number in stock, number sold in current period, number on order from supplier, and reorder level. The stock file may be printed out regularly to show the latest stock and sales and the recommended order quantity for each item.

The operator first enters a customer number, which is validated against a file containing acceptable numbers. The operator then enters the item number and the quantity of each item ordered. The machine retrieves detailed information on the stock file held on disk, multiplies the quantity by the stored price, and displays the results. If an item is out of stock, an out-of-stock indicator is displayed instead of a value. The operator is given the option of satisfying part of an order, recording back orders, substituting another item, or canceling the entry.

After the last order has been processed, totals are printed for checking. These totals can be programmed to suit any requirement. A typical system might incorporate a number of subtotals, entry of a delivery charge, and a final total showing the amount due.

Facilities also exist for inserting new stock items, deleting discontinued stock items, altering prices, and requesting a printout of the stock and sales of any item at any time. Orders on suppliers can be entered into the system and displayed on the screen.

The system is modular in structure and is flexible enough to handle many extensions and alterations. For example, it is possible to print a formatted invoice with a customer's name and address, along with calculations of discounts, special charges, and sales tax. Customer acknowledgments and packing and dispatching documents for warehouse and distribution use can also be printed on local or remote terminals. In addition, manual "override" facilities are provided for handling special types of orders.

Other features include facilities for maintaining back orders, keeping comprehensive stock and sales history files, forecasting sales, and calculating recommended order quantities (using more advanced techniques such as exponential smoothing). The system can also maintain salesmen's files, calculate commissions, and print cumulative sales figures over any period.

The system incorporates sales, purchase, and general ledger subsystems and can generate customer account reports and profitability reports by product line, customer, or salesman. CLAUDIUS can also be connected via telephone lines to a large central computer to extend the processing power of the system.

### Controls and Security

The CLAUDIUS system incorporates a full range of accounting controls, including:

- Documented batch controls on input.
- Audit trail, tracing the path of all transactions through initial validation to the updating of master files.
- Control totals for all computer files, which are checked by the computer programs and printed for clerical inspection.
- Use of double entry for all accounting transactions.
- A range of totaling and subtotaling facilities for all output reports.

The system also offers the following security features:

- A two-level password system to restrict initial access and subsequent access to selected information.
- A grandfather-father-son file copy procedure to protect all master files.
- "Protected" programs, which cannot be amended during operation.

## System Installation

CLAUDIUS can be installed on a turnkey basis. The installation process is normally conducted in four stages, as described below.

### *Stage 1: Survey of Requirements*

A survey of the user's requirements, including a brief review of client operations, is conducted to determine the applicability to CLAUDIUS. The survey studies present procedures, confirms that the software meets basic requirements, identifies nonstandard requirements, and determines whether the computer hardware capabilities (such as available on-line file storage and the number of video-display terminals) meet the requirements of the client. The survey also provides management with firm proposals on systems features and costs and an implementation timetable.

### *State 2: Customization*

When the client has requirements not provided by the standard CLAUDIUS system, it may be necessary to make program changes. This customization will involve determining the required input transactions, inquiry facilities, methods of calculation and processing, and sizes of files and field lengths; defining printed reports; preparing the specifications for all necessary changes to the standard CLAUDIUS system; and making all necessary amendments to the programs.

### *State 3: Systems Installation*

Installation covers all the work between approval of the design and introduction of the new system. The work includes installing hardware, conducting system tests, training management and operating personnel, revising clerical procedures when necessary, and ordering special forms. Additional steps in installation involve converting existing

records to the new system, converting to the new system, and
delivering operating manuals to the user.

### Stage 4: Post-installation Support

Post-installation support involves monitoring the new system to ensure that it is working effectively. This stage may
therefore include reviewing the performance of the system in
terms of order turnaround, stock holding, debtor balances;
providing additional training; and making any necessary
changes in procedures and programs.

The turnkey approach is beneficial to both software supplier
and customer. The supplier's skill and experience ensure that
the system, when installed, will fit smoothly into the customer's business operations and fulfill its expectations. The
customer can look to a single source that is committed to
solving its problems. Under the turnkey system approach, the
supplier provides professional services in addition to
software. The approach is consequently more costly, on the
surface, than a system in which the supplier furnishes only
software and the buyer must do the installation. Large organizations with experienced data processing staffs regularly
purchase or develop software and do their own installation.
Small businesses that are first-time users of a computer system
often find the turnkey approach better suited to their needs.

# 3 JOE HAMILTON

# A Small Business Installs a Microprocessor System

*The following article describes the history of the relationship between a small Iowa farm machinery distributor and the equally small company that furnished it with a microcomputer accounting system. The article provides a detailed description of the distributor's accounting system prior to introduction of the microcomputer as well as a description of how the computer system now works.*

*This is not light reading, but the article gives potential systems buyers an excellent feeling for the process that they and their suppliers will have to follow, the kinds of information they will need to obtain about their business, and the experiences they and their staff will encounter during acquisition and shakedown of the new system.*

JOE HAMILTON is President, Microprocessor Applications, Pella, Iowa. This article was written especially for this book.

**The Farm Machinery Business**

FAGA Implement, Inc., of Adair, Iowa, sells and services John Deere farm machinery. Over the 16-year history of the company under its present owner, Danny Faga, volume has climbed from $104,000 to over $3 million. In 1976, a feasibility study was performed by Dealer Consulting and Data Services of Deere & Company to recommend alternatives to the company's manual accounting procedures. As a result of this study, a microprocessor-based computer system marketed by Microprocessor Applications of Le Mars, Iowa, was installed in June 1977.

Adair is located in southwest Iowa, approximately 50 miles west of Des Moines, where the local economy is dominated by agriculture. The company is distributor for the Deere & Company line of farm implements, serving primarily an area within a 25-mile radius of Adair. For Faga Implement, service after the sale of new or used equipment is of equal importance to the sale itself, and a significant portion of the company is devoted to sales of replacement parts, customer service, and consumer products.

Danny Faga entered the implement business in October of 1962, when he assumed operation of the then Emgarten Implement store. Of his entry into the company, he says, "I started with $11: $1 to bind the contract, and $10 for the cash register." In 1962, a typical family farm operation was 160 acres; an 80-horsepower tractor to handle the heavy work cost about $5,000; and Faga Implement's gross sales were $104,000. There were 3 employees in the business and the physical plant consisted of an antiquated 2,400-square-foot shop building and 4 city lots for machinery. In contrast, today's average farm is nearing 450 acres; the heavy work may require a 250-horsepower tractor, which costs approximately $60,000; and Faga Implement is grossing over $3 million a year. Operations have moved into a new 13,300-square-foot building on a 5-acre lot, and a staff of 20 serves the needs of the farm operators.

## The Old Accounting System

The accounting function of the company has increased in greater proportion to its growth in sales. In the early years of the business, Mr. Faga personally recorded the accounting data. He now, however, employs a full-time bookkeeper and a full-time secretary who also serves as bookkeeper's assistant. Their manual accounting system, which began as a simple cash receipts journal, now embodies:

- Accounts receivable
- Purchases and disbursements
- General ledger
- Payroll
- Parts inventory
- Whole goods inventory

When Mr. Faga began to consider a computer-based accounting system, the various accounting functions were performed as described in the following summaries.

### Accounts Receivable

The accounts receivable were maintained via a subsidiary ledger card system. Of the 600 accounts in the file, approximately 300 were active each month. Changes to the accounts in the form of machinery and parts sales, customer service, consumer products, or payments were recorded on sales tickets, which were processed daily by the bookkeeper. Entries which referenced accounts receivable were posted to the accounts receivable ledger. One card was maintained for each customer in the ledger, and the posting process involved pulling the customer account card, entering the new charge or credit, computing the new balance, and replacing the card in the file. Control totals to the general ledger were compiled on the daily cash receipts and sales journal and entered into the general ledger. The accounts receivable ledger was reconciled twice monthly and an aged trial balance was generated monthly. Statements to active accounts were prepared by photocopying the ledger cards. The process of maintaining accounts receivable required approximately 3 hours each day; reconciling and aging the accounts required about 3 hours, and preparation of statements approximately 8 hours, twice monthly.

An accurate accounts receivable file was maintained. However, Mr. Faga felt that improvements could be achieved in the following areas by utilizing a computer:

1. The daily maintenance of accounts receivable ledger cards manually required much time, and an automated system would allow the bookkeeper to spend more time performing managerial duties.
2. Statements would be prepared more efficiently.
3. Service charges were not posted to the ledger, but rather were computed when the statements were generated. An automated system would easily prepare service charge transactions and post them immediately to the accounts receivable ledger.

### Purchases and Disbursements

Approximately 330 invoices were processed each month by the bookkeeper. Outstanding invoices were paid twice monthly unless a discount could be obtained by earlier remittance. Invoice data was entered in a purchases and disbursements journal when the invoice was to be paid. As with accounts receivable, a subsidiary ledger card system was maintained. Approximately 100 vendor accounts were active each month. Since all invoices were paid within 30 days, the bookkeeper did not enter invoices into the accounts payable account when they were received. In this respect, a current accounts payable balance was not readily available on demand. Also, no regular cash requirements reports were generated for management.

By automating the purchases and disbursements function via an accounts payable system, Mr. Faga expected improvements in:

1. Cash requirements reporting.
2. More efficient balancing and entry into the general ledger.
3. Time required for maintaining the file by elimination of the ledger cards.

## General Ledger

Faga Implement is a participant in the Deere & Company Dealer Management Program. This program establishes standards for the general accounting function and assists the dealer in financial statement preparation. Under the program, the following exhibits and journals were prepared according to standards recommended by Deere & Company:

- Chart of accounts
- Cash receipts and sales journal
- Purchases and disbursements journal
- General journal
- Employee earnings records
- Balance sheet

At the end of each accounting period, the bookkeeper completed several exhibits, which were submitted to Deere & Company for processing. The data from these exhibits were entered onto computer-based files and collated with historical data for Faga Implement and other participating dealers of comparable size. Then several summary reports were generated for management use at the dealership. The reports compared the dealership's past month's performance with previous months and years for the dealer and for other comparable stores.

The primary elements of the exhibits prepared for Faga Implement by the Dealer Management Program were:

- Balance sheet
- Return on investment
- Return on assets
- Parts turnover

- Breakeven point
- Accounts receivable aging
- Departmental summary of income, expense, and profit
- Other miscellaneous statistics

These reports were a valuable tool for Mr. Faga to utilize in measuring the company's progress over both the short and long term. Therefore, Mr. Faga did not want to relinquish this service if a computer-based accounting system was installed.

The daily cash receipts and sales journal consumed most of the bookkeeper's time with the general ledger. This journal was created from the sales tickets for the previous day's business. After balancing and reconciling cash, totals from this journal were entered into the general ledger.

The general journal was used for entry of depreciation, taxes, insurance, and year-end adjustments. Approximately 2 to 3 hours per day were spent maintaining these two journals.

Mr. Faga's expectation was that utilizing a computer for accounting would provide improvements in:

1. Amount of time spent journalizing, especially the cash receipts and sales journal.
2. Automatic transfer of control totals from the subsidiary ledgers to the general ledger.
3. More efficient generation of daily and end-of-period reports.

### Payroll

Employee earnings records were maintained for each employee of the company. Sales, parts, customer service, and office employees were on a fixed hourly rate with weekly pay periods. The owner was paid a fixed salary, which was prepared bimonthly. Several employees were also participants in a commission plan in addition to their regular wages. Approximately 2½ hours per week were required for the bookkeeper to prepare the employee checks, update the employee earnings records, and record the checks in the purchases and disbursements journal.

Although the bookkeeper performed the payroll function efficiently, the sheer number of computations required in preparation of tax and commission data and updating the employee earnings records indicated that using a computer system would save time.

### Parts Inventory

Parts inventory was performed on the central computer system at Deere & Company. Each day, a parts department employee, using the sales tickets and inventory adjustment forms, would punch a paper tape of the previous day's parts sales on a teletypewriter. The Deere & Company computer would then poll the teletype during the night and process the tape. After collating the data with the dealer's parts inventory master file, a new inventory listing would be generated weekly and replacement parts ordered. The inventory system also generated several valuable management reports, including:

- Obsolete items
- Slow-moving items
- Total dollar amounts sold by the parts and service departments
- Total warranty parts
- Inventory, both net current and total
- Comparisons to other dealers of comparable size
- Miscellaneous statistics

Since Deere & Company could more efficiently identify slow-moving and obsolete items, prepare return lists, and reorder items, Mr. Faga wished to remain with this system instead of using an in-house computer file. Doing so also significantly reduced the minimum machine size required for the other accounting functions.

## Whole Goods Inventory

The accounting of whole goods inventory had been a recordkeeping problem for the company. After several unsuccessful systems were tried, an inventory method using a machinery book was implemented. This book was updated daily from sales tickets and invoices. A tag number was assigned to each machine and attachment, thus facilitating easier identification of items.

Although this method was working, a computer-based system would be capable of providing:

1. More efficient reconciliation of totals to the general ledger.
2. Computation of "washout" for new and used machines which involved trade-ins.
3. Actual cost of used equipment.

## Planning the New Computer System

Mr. Faga enlisted the aid of Deere & Company's Dealer Consulting and Data Services to perform a data processing survey for his company. Dealer Consulting and Data Services is a department within Deere & Company consisting of business professionals capable of solving problems by recommending procedures to be used in the dealer organization for processing information. Of such a service, Mr. Faga says, "Occasionally the small businessman requires advice from professionals outside the immediate organization to help in planning and programming. The people at Dealer Consulting were very helpful in providing a professional and unbiased study for my consideration. Their work reflected adherence to Deere & Company policies while remaining sensitive to my individual needs as an independent dealer."

The data processing survey was performed during the fourth quarter of 1976. Based upon the results of the survey, Dealer Consulting concluded that the mechanization of several application areas was feasible. They recommended the automation of accounts receivable, accounts payable, payroll, general ledger, and whole goods inventory. Upon reviewing the study with them, Mr. Faga concurred that a move to an electronic data processing system would be beneficial to the organization.

Once the decision was made to mechanize, the next problem was to find a company which would serve the dealer's needs at an affordable price. If a computer was to be successfully utilized, it had to be:

1. A complete turnkey installation.
2. Reliable.
3. Simple enough to be operated by a person with no prior computer experience.
4. Less expensive than hiring a person to perform equivalent work.
5. Compatible with Deere & Company's standards to allow continuation of participation in their Dealer Management Program.

Three companies were reviewed as possible vendors by Dealer Consulting. Of those, Faga Implement selected Microprocessor Applications from Le Mars, Iowa. This company was the only one which could provide the services outlined for a price Mr. Faga deemed reasonable. In addition, Mr. Faga had a personal relationship with the company's managers and had worked with them earlier in discussions about another computer project.

**Implementing the System**

Microprocessor Applications (commonly known as Micro-Ap) began operation in 1976 with a goal of providing a turnkey small business computer system for under $10,000. To achieve this goal, the company employed a practice that was rare at that time: using low-cost microprocessors for general data processing applications. The microprocessor unit itself proved capable of maneuvering data fast enough to provide the system with a good nucleus. The problem was with peripheral equipment. The printers, video-keyboard terminals, tape, and diskette units which were established in the marketplace were designed for use by minicomputers and were prohibitively expensive. Microprocessor Applications had to find more competitive peripheral equipment.

After an extensive search, a system was drawn together which was capable of processing accounting applications. Its primary components were:

1. An Intel 8080A microprocessor provided with support circuitry, power supply, and cabinet by IMS Associates, Inc., of California.
2. A 20,000-character main memory.
3. A tape cassette interface from Tarbell Electronics of California.
4. Four audio cassette tape units.
5. A keyboard from Cherry Electronics of Illinois.
6. A video display from Processor Technology of California.
7. An electrosensitive printer from Axiom of California.

While selection of hardware was difficult, developing the programs proved to be even more of a problem. The software literally had to be built from the ground up. The only software available to the company was a simple assembler language for the 8080A and several limited versions of basic language interpreters. The company decided to initially implement the programs using assembler language. The company's president describes his decision: "I thought that if I could develop a good subroutine package in assembler language that could also be used later by a higher-level compiler language, then over the long term the software would be more easily implemented and execute faster than if basic was used. Although basic would be superior for some small programs, I did not want the company to become 'locked into' it, since BASIC is a very poor language to use for accounting and reporting applications."

The Micro-Ap computer system was installed at Faga Implement in June of 1977, and the first application went into use within two months. The system currently performs accounts receivable, accounts payable, general ledger, and payroll. It is designed for use by persons with no prior experience with computers. Faga Implement's bookkeeper, JoAnn Morris, has been operating the machine since its installation and has been key to its successful implementation. Of her involvement in the project, Sam Hamilton, hardware specialist, indicates: "Although we are proud of the system's performance, there were some bugs in the hardware and software which did not become visible until she began using it on a daily basis. She understood that, as it was one of our prototype installations, we were all experimenting with something new, and her helpfulness had been appreciated."

## How the System Operates

The computer interacts with the operator through use of the keyboard and video display. The program displays data formats and instructions, and the operator responds through the keyboard. This simplifies the data entry process and facilitates the machine's use by less experienced operators. All procedures which require manual intervention, such as tape loading, are prompted by instructions displayed on the video display. When possible, error detection is performed at the time the data is entered, and error messages prompt the operator when necessary. When a journal is being created, the total debits and credits for each document are tallied and displayed, and the data is not accepted until it balances. In addition, journal totals are accumulated throughout the process and available for immediate display.

All data entered for the accounts receivable, general ledger, accounts payable, and other functions is captured by the same program. This program allows entry of any combination of the following operations to be performed during one execution: general journal; accounts payable (purchases and disbursements) journal; cash receipts and sales journal; and additions, changes, or deletions to general ledger, accounts receivable, or accounts payable. Switching from one operation to another is very simple, allowing the total data entry for the day to be done at once.

Once the data is entered and balanced to the bookkeeper's satisfaction, programs are initiated by the operator to print the journals, sort the transaction data, and post to the particular ledger files. Posting the data to the appropriate ledgers requires sorting the current day's entries and executing a posting program for each of the three ledgers. All master and transaction data is stored on a single file for a particular ledger, which simplifies the posting and reporting process. Since posting involves creating a new file from the previous master file data and the current day's transactions, backup copies of all the ledger files are always available if problems should arise.

Once the data is posted, the operator simply initiates programs to produce any reports which are needed. Reports available from the system are:

- Cash receipts and sales journal
- General journal
- Purchases and disbursements journal
- Accounts receivable journal
- General ledger
- Accounts receivable ledger
- Accounts payable ledger
- Check register
- Cash requirements report
- Purchase order encumbrance report
- Vendor report
- Accounts receivable statements of account
- Trial balances (available for all ledgers)
- Accounts receivable aged trial balance

- Financial statements
- Miscellaneous reports

Among the more unique features of the accounting package are the ability of the financial statement programs to work with variable format exhibits and the capability of accounts payable and general ledger systems to process encumbrances. The payroll function involves maintenance of the employee earnings records on tape file and automatic computation of most period payroll data.
The data stored on the accounting system files are:

- General ledger chart of accounts—account number, department number, description
- General ledger budget entry—account number, department number, balances forward for budget, encumbrance, expense, and prior year
- General ledger transaction—account number, department number, date, source journal, reference, description, amount, debit/credit code, column code (budget, encumbrance, etc.)
- Accounts receivable master information—identification number, name, address, type, credit rating; balances forward for current, 30 days, 60 days, and 90 days past due; credit limit
- Accounts receivable transaction—identification number, date, source journal, reference, description, amount, debit/credit code
- Accounts payable vendor information—identification number, name, address, type, year-to-date, total paid
- Accounts payable encumbrance transaction—identification number, date, source journal, reference, line number, general ledger account and department number, description, amount, debit/credit code
- Accounts payable invoice transaction—identification number, date, source journal, reference, line number,

general ledger account and department number, description, amount, discount, status, pay date

Several additional applications for use by Faga Implement are being developed. Among these are the whole goods inventory programs, long-range planning, and general business statistical package. The long-range planning program allows the user to develop models of various functions and characteristics of the organization and the environment in which it operates. Once the model is developed and tested against historical data, alternative projections of the model may be performed by altering the manner in which the variables change and interact within the model over several time periods. An example would be changing short-term loan interest rates within an overhead projection model and measuring their effect on net income. If a plan has been carefully built by the manager who understands the interaction of the pieces of the plan, extremely useful data can be extracted via a "what if" approach or projection.

Based upon Danny Faga's experience of conversion to electronic data processing using a microcomputer, he offers the following advice: "The manager should either develop a trust in the computer salesman or hire a consultant to select the system. Most of us are not knowledgeable enough about alternative hardware and software to make an intelligent comparison. Above all, adopt an attitude of 'hanging on to your pocketbook.' The entry of microprocessors into our market is an important factor concerning system cost. In many respects, small companies like mine have the same computational problems as the large companies, yet we don't have the capital to invest in a large computer system. In conclusion, a successful implementation of a computer system in the small business depends largely upon the vendor's marketing and technical personnel understanding your needs and providing the same service your clientele expects from you."

# 4 RANDALL RUSTIN

# The Microcomputer in Action: Support of Loan Collection

*Large businesses are just as interested as small businesses in taking advantage of the convenience and reduced costs of microcomputers. The following article describes how one of the nation's largest banks switched from a large computer to a microcomputer system.*

*The legal department of the bank maintains files of documents on each of the many debt collection cases normally under litigation. For some time, the bank had been using a commercial time-sharing service to maintain its files. The bank's personnel had written the programs that controlled this computer application, and the bank was paying the time-sharing company and the telephone company*

RANDALL RUSTIN is a consultant in New York City. This article was written especially for this book.

regular monthly fees for processing and for communications between the bank and the computer.

The bank's legal department became concerned about the continuation of these costs. The monthly charges were substantial, rising with general increases in prices, and would continue as long as the system was used. The bank accordingly decided to obtain its own computer for this application. The one-time expense of a dedicated microcomputer (a system devoted to a single application) was not great, and elimination of the recurring outside service costs made justification easy. Confidentiality of data was, of course, improved. The system was installed and is operating successfully.

Most of the microcomputer systems described in this book involve financial and accounting applications. In this case, the microcomputer is being used to support a "production" function—scheduling and coordinating the steps involved in processing legal cases. The many parallels to "production" functions in other kinds of businessess are not hard to find.

This case also illustrates the growing movement away from shared use of centralized computer systems to decentralized or distributed processing.

## Introduction

THE bank's Legal Department is charged with the collection of debts referred by any area of the bank. Thus, the bank is the plaintiff and the Legal Department's mandate is the collection of the defaulted loans. The collection procedure is lengthy and may be complicated in many ways by the actions taken by the debtors and the responses to those actions taken by the bank.

Whether or not the case enters litigation, there is an extensive sequence of legal documents generated at specific times, sent to specific places, and recorded as part of each case's history. The system automates the document preparation, recordkeeping, event monitoring, bookkeeping, and management reporting associated with the plaintiff activities performed by the Legal Department.

The application had been implemented on a large remote computer, accessible from a terminal in the Legal Department. Legal Department management, though basically pleased with the functional capabilities of the system, had become increasingly concerned with its high operating costs. These costs were charges for computer processing time, data base storage, document printing, communication lines, and the use of a generalized report-writing package.

In addition to the difficulty imposed by the growing costs, there were difficulties resulting from the need to employ consultants to deal with much of the off-site operation and programming. Unable to bear these costs, the Legal Department called upon an advanced technology group within the bank for assistance. After thorough study of the situation this group proposed, designed, and implemented a microcomputer system functionally equivalent to the original system. This microcomputer system, its mode of operation, and the functions that it performs are the subject of this paper.

## The Microcomputer System

The system hardware is comprised of a microprocessor, primary and secondary storage media and input–output facilities. A more detailed list with approximate prices appears in the table below:

| | |
|---|---:|
| Z-80 microprocessor with chassis | $ 1,800 |
| 64,000 characters of random-access memory (RAM) | 2,400 |
| 1 video monitor | 600 |
| 1 printer | 3,200 |
| 4 diskette drives with interface and controller | 4,700 |
| 1 cathode ray tube (CRT) terminal with keyboard | 1,600 |
| 40 diskettes | 200 |
| Software: operating system, data base management, and debugging system | 500 |
| Total | $15,000 |
| | |
| Service contract at 15% of total cost | $2,250/year |

The microcomputer system has none of the operating costs described above for the pre-existing system. There are no communications, operating system, or storage charges. There are no remote aspects: it is a dedicated, on-premises computer system. The configuration fits entirely into a secretary's work station. The system's operator is the user. It is functionally equivalent (actually somewhat more powerful) to the original system. The total of the hardware and system development cost was approximately $50,000.

## System Operation Mode

Data is entered through the typewriter keyboard of the video display unit. Anything typed will appear, appropriately formatted, on the display screen. Input data and queries are all entered at this station. The end user, the legal investigator or a suitable paralegal aide, is the actual operator of the system.

Requests, or queries, are made by selecting functions from the "menu" appearing on the display screen. When more information is necessary to execute a function, the computer prompts by issuing instructions to the operator, who then enters more data. All functions are initiated from a menu called the "main menu." This menu appears at system startup. All the possible user functions appear in the menu. Figure 1 is a reproduction of this display. Since each function is numbered, the user simply types the number corresponding to the desired function. The system then responds by replacing the main menu with another menu, which lists subfunctions, or actions, that the operator must fulfill in order to effect the function.

Figure 2 is the menu display corresponding to the third function, "Document Definition," in the main menu. This menu lists the sequence of actions that the operator must fulfill in order to define a document. This involves typing particular values of data. These values will appear on the screen so that the operator may verify their correctness. A

**Figure 1.**

```
MAIN MENU:

INVESTIGATOR: _____

FUNCTIONS:

    1.  CASE INPUT
    2.  CASE UPDATE
    3.  DOCUMENT DEFINITION FILE: MAINTENANCE
    4.  DAILY INVESTIGATOR REPORT
    5.  CASE ACTION/DOCUMENT REQUEST UPDATE
    6.  DOCUMENT REQUEST FILE PRINT/UPDATE
    7.  DOCUMENT GENERATION
    8.  CASE DB PRINT
    9.  MIS REPORTS
   10.  DAILY TRANSACTION LOG
   11.  PRINT FOLDER LABELS
   12.  RETURN TO THE OPERATING SYSTEM

ENTER FUNCTION NUMBER OR "I" TO CHANGE
INVESTIGATOR CODE _____
```

**Figure 2.**

```
DOCUMENT DEFINITION MENU – 3

    1.  PRINT DOCUMENT DEFINITIONS
    2.  ADD DOCUMENT DEFINITION LINE
    3.  DELETE DOCUMENT DEFINITION LINE
    4.  ADD SELECTOR FIELD
    5.  DELETE SELECTOR FIELD
    6.  UPDATE SELECTOR FIELD

ENTER FUNCTION NUMBER _____
```

certain amount of validation of format types—i.e., alphabetic, numeric, etc.—is performed by the system.

When a document has been constructed internally by the system it can be displayed on the screen or can be immediately produced by the system printer. This is an operator option, although most documents appear directly as printed output.

There are over 50 different document types produced by the system. Many of them are standard letters with particular changing fields—as, for example, name, address, account number, account balance, etc. The system's data management facilities retrieve and insert the appropriate values in the pre-formatted text. Many of the documents are preprinted forms—as, for example, summons, judgment, etc. For these, the system inserts values in appropriate places on the pages.

When different forms must be inserted into the printer, or different diskettes mounted in the disk drives, the system prompts the operator for the appropriate forms. After a diskette is loaded the system checks the correct identifying label on the diskette, informs the operator of any discrepancies, and holds back execution until the corrections are made.

### System Functions

The system contains several principal groups of user functions; they are the Data Base Management, Document Generation, Bookkeeping, Management Reporting, and Event Monitoring Functions. They are initiated by the operator using CRT terminal commands. Underlying the general user functions are more specific system functions, which are illustrated in Figure 3.

### *Function Overview*

The most important production function of the system is the automatic, or semiautomatic, generation of the legal documents required in the steps of the plaintiff case process. The operator may specify the documents to be produced by use of commands and parameters. The Legal Document Generation Functions locate the required data from the data base, produce all required fields for the document, and print the desired number of copies in the desired format.

To support the Legal Document Generation Functions, and to provide accurate monetary payment data, the Bookkeeping Functions access the data base and compute the necessary balances for each case.

The Management Reporting Functions provide statistical reports for assisting in the management of case processing.

The Event Monitoring Functions keep track of case processing history and provide a calendar of events to be performed for each case. At operator request, Event Monitoring Reports for each investigator can be issued. The report by date (or range of dates) is used to remind each investigator of the necessary case actions to be taken that day.

### Document Preparation

Documents produced are either legal documents, letters using Legal Department conventions, or reports. The system is able to generate several different types of legal documents based on operator-entered parameters and data. Upon operator request of the Document Generation Functions, the system provides a CRT prompt for the selection of the designated document and case involved. The system then prompts the operator to enter the necessary parameters and input data. The system performs field validity checks after the data is entered. The document parameters contain selection criteria specifying the desired number of copies and the variable data to be printed on the document.

The document generation process involves determining the required data elements, retrieving the elements from the data base, computing any derived data, processing as determined from the input parameters, formatting all printed

**Figure 3.**

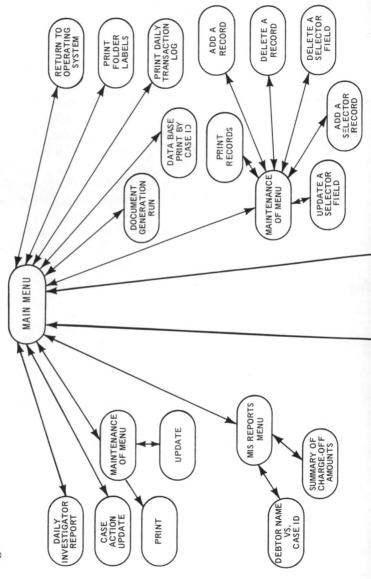

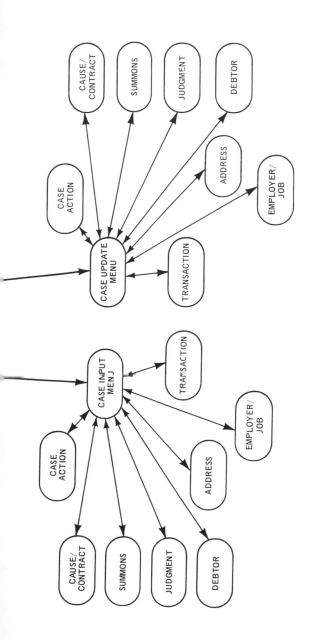

fields, prompting the mounting of appropriate forms, and completing the printing.

### Management Reporting Functions

The system produces management reports reflecting the status of active cases—as, for example, the following:

- For every investigator, print out the status of all cases for which that investigator is responsible. This includes the number of cases closed for a given period, the balances for each open case, the names of debtors for each case, etc.
- For each outside collector, give monthly or quarterly summaries (with dollar amounts) of running year-to-date statistics on number of cases allotted and still active. (Outside collectors are agents who handle cases referred to them by the bank.)

### Bookkeeping Functions

The system performs all of the bookkeeping functions involved in loan collection, and computation of all financial data used in document preparation.

### Event Monitoring

The system provides an event monitoring capability for every case in the system. For each case the system stores a "past" and "next" action. The past action is the last activity involving the case. Based on the past action, the system will automatically store the next action and the date when it must occur. For those activities that have no automatic next action, the system operator may prescribe the next activity with its associated time, by specifying the case ID, the next action, and the number of intervening days. The operator may also override the next action assigned by the system.

## Conclusion

The system automates the recordkeeping, document preparation, event monitoring, bookkeeping, and management reporting associated with the plaintiff activities performed by the Legal Department. The primary innovative aspect of the system is the fact that it is microcomputer-based. This resulted in considerably lower implementation and operating costs, and certain other definite advantages.

The system is owned by, and completely dedicated to, the Legal Department. This permits much greater control of the hardware and of data which is considered private or "sensitive." (Privacy of data is particularly an issue in a Legal Department.) It should be noted that a microcomputer system is not the only computer system that can be dedicated in house; minicomputer systems share the same advantage. However, minis, besides being larger and much more expensive, usually require support equipment that of itself may create problems. For example, most minicomputers require an air-conditioned environment and relatively large power supplies. The microcomputer system requires no special air-conditioning and power requirements. It is as simple to install and to maintain as, for example, high-fidelity equipment.

# 5

# The Most Current—
# The Least Expensive

There is almost no limit to the ways microcomputers can help small businesses improve their operations and bottom-line results. Ingenuity is not in short supply either. Many businesses have successfully developed individualized systems, buying equipment from computer stores and writing their own programs.

This section provides brief descriptions of six successful microcomputer installations. They cover a wide variety of businesses: from a plumbing contractor to a beer distributor to an amusement park. In most cases, the users developed their own programs. None of the five users could have afforded a larger computer, and only the very low cost of the microcomputer encouraged them to proceed. The descriptions of these installations gives an excellent idea of how other businesses are benefiting from microcomputers and how they went about developing and installing their own business systems.

All the descriptions were furnished to the editors by the Pertec Computer Corporation of Los Angeles, Cal., whose microsystems division manufactures the MITS/Altair™ microcomputer product line. They were prepared in March 1978 and are reprinted by permission of Simon/Public Relations, Inc., Los Angeles, Cal.

## A CREDIT UNION

GIANT, expensive computers are a mainstay of operations in banks and savings and loan associations. But what about a credit union with only 300 members, a much overworked volunteer treasurer, and a budget that allows for only one full-time employee?

Computerization was necessary, reports Bill Mashburn, who's in charge of systems and security for the Rockwell (N.C.) Federal Credit Union. But the credit union couldn't afford a big computer or even a minicomputer. Rockwell's time-sharing system was available only at inconvenient hours, and employing an outside time-sharing service also was too expensive.

The answer to the credit union's problem: a $7,000 microcomputer, one of the new desk-top computing systems that have come on the market in recent years.

Mashburn and his fellow credit union members all are employees at the flow control division of Rockwell International, Los Angeles. The division, which has 400 employees, is a major supplier of high-pressure steam valves.

The credit union's microcomputer—a MITS/Altair 8800A, manufactured and marketed by Pertec Computer Corporation Microsystems Division, Chatsworth, Cal.—went into operation the first of this year.

"With the limited funds available to our 300-member organization, we had to look very closely at how we could computerize effectively on our kind of budget," Mashburn recalls. "First we tried to see if we could utilize Rockwell's own time-sharing system—but it was so busy we could only get on it at about 1:00 or 2:00 in the morning.

"For a time we thought of going onto an outside time-sharing service with another credit union in town, but to do only a small amount of work was still over $100 a month. And to have to send all our paperwork out, we felt, was just too much hassle for volunteer labor.

"I looked at several minicomputers next, and listened to

their salesmen, but believe it or not those machines—at a far higher price—didn't do half what our present system will do," Mashburn continues. . . . "Finally I began calling computer clubs all over the country and asking a lot of questions about which systems were best. At that time I didn't really know much about computers and had never built one, but one enthusiast I spoke to convinced me that MITS was the way to go, and that I could in fact build one myself from a kit.

"So I went before the credit union's board of directors and presented my case, and they decided to get it: a total cost for the system of about $7,000, which we amortized over three years—that's a little less than $10 per member."

Rockwell Credit Union's system, purchased in kit form at Microsystems, the Altair Computer Center in Arlington, Va., consists of a MITS/Altair 8800A mainframe with 32K bytes of memory; one disk drive; a Lear-Siegler ADM-3 video display terminal; and a Centronics 701 printer with 60-character-per-second printing speed.

Mashburn and his staff opted to do all programming rather than buy ready-made programs. "You can buy the accounting package," he explains, "but we felt it would be advantageous to write our own program that would be tailored to our specific job."

In operation, the computer system's disk storage unit is initially loaded with the data on all member accounts. Then, at the end of the day each time the credit union is open (twice a week), the office manager keys in all transactions that have occurred that day, to update the disk.

"She calls up the account, the account information is displayed on the CRT screen, and she updates that piece of information," Mashburn explains. "Then the printer prints out what the transaction was, for the journal and cash record, and she goes on to the next account.

"After working through the day's transactions, balancing and checking for errors, she then has the computer print out a 'working sheet' for use during the next day's business—a list showing the current status of everybody's account, one account per line, for the entire credit union. This print operation takes about five to ten minutes.

"Also, we pay dividends quarterly, so at the end of each quarter we'll have the computer calculate dividends and add them to each account, and print out statement sheets for everybody. Until now we've had to calculate each member's dividends individually, type up his account sheet, and make a photocopy of the sheet to send him. When you use volunteer labor—our office manager who operates the computer is our only paid employee—the time saved here means a lot.

"Of course, we haven't had much experience with the system yet," Mashburn adds, "but we're really hoping it will reduce the workload of our volunteer treasurer, in particular. I think we're getting a good deal for our money, though we did put a lot of hours of labor into building it—if we had bought this as a turnkey hardware system it would probably have come to about $10,000 instead of $7,000. Still, I've been keeping my eyes open and so far I haven't found another system on the market that can do what this one does for anywhere near the price we paid for it."

## A BEER DISTRIBUTOR

A microcomputer is helping Coors Northeast, a Houston wholesale beer distributor, compile meaningful sales reports that have helped the firm to boost its sales.

The company, which distributes one million cases of brew a year to taverns and stores in its territory, used to have to wait two weeks for monthly sales reports that compare results on different types of accounts, ethnic areas and demographic sectors, together with comparisons with results of the previous month and of the same month last year.

Salespeople then could spot sales downturns and other developments, but it often was too late to do anything about them.

A year ago, Coors Northeast bought a MITS microcomputer system and developed its own software for route accounting. Now, the monthly sales statistics are whipped out in four hours, and Coors Northeast can dispatch salespeople "where they're needed—and now," reports Vincent Polichino, Operations Manager.

"We're able to see results from targeted work in the field, see what's happening out there right away, and send in people *now*," he says. "This has helped us boost sales substantially."

In addition, the system handles daily route accounting, reconciling sales and inventory, checking each driver's settlement sheet (what he took out versus what he returned with) and computing cash from sales.

The system has worked out so well that Coors Northeast now is offering to sell it to other Coors distributors, with Burcon, Inc., the Houston MITS distributor, supplying hardware and the beer wholesaler supplying software.

While thus far the system has been used as a sales tool, Coors Northeast also has purchased a general ledger software package developed by Altair Software Development Company and soon will buy a payroll package from ASDC. Adding those two functions is expected to create labor savings.

The hardware that Coors Northeast acquired is comprised of a MITS/Altair 8800B CPU (48K of core memory) with three floppy disk drives, an LSI ADM-3 video terminal, and a Texas Instruments 810 high-speed printer. It acquired this from Burcon, one of 40 distributors of MITS microcomputer products.

The desk-top hardware cost about $12,500, and Polichino wrote the route accounting software package himself for about $8,000. Compared to that, he notes, a minicomputer system for the same task would have cost between $35,000 and $50,000.

Coors Northeast has 10 routes, and when its truck drivers complete their travels each morning, data from each of their sales tickets is entered into the system—some 300 entries daily. By 10 A.M., management has a complete report on the day's sales, also reconciled with inventory. This report previously wasn't available until late afternoon.

Polichino notes that inputting data to the route accounting system takes a bit longer than with the old manual approach, but "we get data out of it ten times faster."

The monthly sales report, which used to take two people two weeks to compile, now is available in four hours. Also, a salesperson can easily inspect any account now, simply by having the video terminal highlight sales "right up to today," says Polichino. Before, the records were on cards, and the salesperson would have to dig through old cards.

Polichino reports no special training procedures were needed to prepare the computer operators. "They spent two to three days watching the procedures, and then worked directly with the computer. It's easy because the terminal prompts them on what input they must do."

## AN AMUSEMENT PARK

Behind the scenes at Knott's Berry Farm in Buena Park, Cal., three small desk-top microcomputers are helping to operate the nation's oldest and third-largest theme amusement park (after Disney World and Disneyland).

The computers are used by the construction and maintenance division in scheduling and expediting the many maintenance and construction jobs continually in progress; lighting control; and air-conditioning control to promote energy conservation.

Knott's Berry Farm, which hosts 4 million visitors a year on its 150 acres—featuring more than 100 rides and attractions, eating places, and unique shops—boasts some of the world's most advanced electronics systems.

Mike Reafsnyder, director of construction and maintenance, long had recognized a growing need for computer support to his division in maintaining the Farm's attractions and, when desired, adding new features. The situation became critical after the Farm opened its "Roaring Twenties" area in 1975 and attendance zoomed by 52 percent.

Given the availability of the division's strong internal electronics department—whose engineers had recently helped to install such "thrill rides" as the Corkscrew and the 20-story Sky Tower parachute jump—Reafsnyder felt confident that his staff could build the needed computerized control systems themselves, starting with computer kits.

The three MITS/Altair 8800 microcomputers that provide the central control for the division's systems were purchased in kit form from the Altair Computer Center in Santa Monica, Cal.

While each of the three microcomputers is dedicated to a specific application (i.e., work order scheduling, lighting, and air conditioning), all the terminals and printers can be switched as needed to any of the three applications. Computer system hardware includes three Ann Arbor terminals, three 110-cps Okidata line printers, and three disk drives. The work order scheduling system uses 40K bytes of mainframe memory; the lighting and air-conditioning systems use 16K and 20K, respectively. Each of the three disk drives uses 300K bytes of floppy disk storage.

Design and implementation of the lighting and air-conditioning control portions of the system, performed under the direction of electronics department supervisor Chuck Linn, entailed the installation of approximately $75,000 worth of acoustically coupled transmission and receiving equipment to control 11 separate lighting areas and approximately 50 air-conditioning units.

Total cost of the computer hardware for the three-part system—excluding the transmission/receiving equipment—was $21,800. Custom programming was performed by a software contractor, Jon Vrooman, at a cost of $10,500. The entire system was installed and operational by December 1976.

The work order expediting system schedules the construction and maintenance division's workload, based on due dates and priorities that have been assigned to the various jobs. When more than one shop is involved in a particular job, the computer takes this into consideration and coordinates the different shops. A printed listing, showing all jobs in priority order, is furnished periodically to the division's various managers.

In the lighting control system, the computer provides centralized control to turn various groups of lights throughout the Farm on and off at prespecified times. Staff assistant Ralph Ruffolo, who oversees the operation of the division's computerized systems, explains: "While we have our regular lighting schedule that remains fairly constant, we can also enter the 'on' and 'off' times for special events that require lighting at unscheduled times—in our theater and wagon camp, for example. Then, after that special event is over, it is purged from the memory and the system reverts to its normal schedule."

All of the Farm's lighting, except a few parking lots and other peripheral areas, is under computer control. "While the lighting is currently divided up into just 11 sections for control purposes, we do intend to break it down more finely in the future," Ruffolo explains. "The system has the capability of controlling up to 100 separate lighting areas."

Primary purpose of the third computerized system now in operation, air conditioning control, is conserving energy and minimizing the Farm's electric utility bills, "The system compares actual kilowatts being used by the entire Farm at any given moment with a 'standard kilowatt' amount that has been designated as a standard for that particular time of day," says Ruffolo. "And whenever the actual kilowatt amount exceeds the standard, various air-conditioning units will begin to cycle off and on at short intervals—usually every ten minutes.

"All the air conditioners on the Farm are grouped into three different priorities," Ruffolo continues, "and the computer automatically searches its memory, finds the air conditioners in the lowest-priority group which are running at the time the signal to begin cycling is received, and will selectively begin to cycle these units. If cycling a major portion of the lowest-priority units does not return power to the standard, the system will begin cycling the next priority group, and will continue this procedure until actual kilowatts return to the standard amount."

One additional feature built into the system guards against excessive "peak" power usage which could adversely affect the Farm's utility rate structure. In the event that power usage should reach a "maximum kilowatt" figure, the system will continue to cycle as before, but will increase the "off" times by 20 percent.

"At present a large part of the Farm's air conditioning is on the computer-controlled system, and we are still in the process of adding more air conditioners to it," Ruffolo points out. "The present system can handle up to 100 individually controlled units—and with about 50 on the system now, we still have a lot of room for expansion.

"We also plan to add another major application to the system in the near future—inventory management," says Ruffolo. "This will help us keep better track of the parts that our various shops need. As shop personnel use up their parts, they'll note this on their daily work cards. We'll key this information into the computer, and it will tell us when we're reaching dangerously low inventory levels. For this, we plan to use MITS/Altair's standard inventory management program."

## A MAIL-ORDER BUSINESS

HELP WANTED: Distributor of fund-raising carnival supplies would like employee who will update, sort, and print 40,000-name mailing list; handle accounts payable bookkeeping; keep track of inventory; and, whenever called on, print shipping labels, type error-free letters, prepare charts, and figure Bingo odds. Will be expected to take on accounts receivable and payroll bookkeeping in future. SALARY: One-time payment only, under $12,000. No salary to be paid thereafter.

S. Lachman & Sons of College Park, Md., didn't actually run this "help wanted" ad—but if it had, the microcomputer system it acquired would have filled the position perfectly.

Gary Cooper, vice president of this fourth-generation family-owned business, explains: "We were buying mailing lists from outside suppliers and doing everything manually. This was very unsatisfactory—the lists we bought were never updated properly and contained many obsolete names and addresses. And with over 40,000 names to keep track of, handling the job manually was terribly inefficient. . . .

The microcomputer, a MITS/Altair 8800B, was purchased as a turnkey hardware system from Microsystems, the Altair Computer Center in Arlington, Va. Total cost of this system configuration—including two disk drives with extensive floppy disk storage capacity, video display terminal, and printer—was in the $10,000–$12,000 range.

Cooper points out, "Our system is a relatively large configuration, and I feel it's comparable in capability to a typical minicomputer system costing four or five times as much."

Lachman supplies materials used in fund-raising events—carnivals, fairs, parties, etc.—put on by such organizations as schools, churches, fire departments, and service clubs. Product lines include everything from Bingo supplies, roulette wheels, and blackjack tables to New Year's hats and horns. However, Lachman only supplies these items to charitable, civic, and religious organizations—not to professional gamblers.

In its mailing list application, the system updates and corrects names and addresses, sorts the names into any desired sequence or category, and prints out pressure-sensitive mailing labels.

"Now, all we have to do is input the names once at the computer terminal—and from that point on it's very simple to write a little program to sort them into any kind of classification we want," says Cooper, "whether it's alphabetically, by zip code, by type of business, or whatever.

"If I want to sort through my 40,000 names and mail only to fire departments in Delaware, the computer can do that. And if I want to compound that with fire departments in Virginia and West Virginia, all I have to do is put in each of those three diskettes for a couple of minutes, and next thing I know the machine has sorted together a brand-new list of fire departments in those three states. I tell the computer to 'sort it' and they're all in zip code order; then I tell it to 'print it' and I've got the labels for a new list, customized for whatever marketing I want to do.

"I get about 2,000 names on each diskette—which means it's costing about 0.5 cent per name for shortage. That's as cheap as keeping the names on labels, and here we can use each name an unlimited number of times and re-sort the names in unlimited different ways."

Lachman's microcomputer also handles the company's accounts payable, replacing a large mechanical bookkeeping machine previously used for this purpose.

"Our computer makes posting a lot faster and doesn't have the maintenance problems of the mechanical system," Cooper says. "All you need to do is key in an account number and it automatically searches the files, gets the account, finds its past balance, asks you the pertinent questions and does all the posting—and when it's all finished, it gives you a hard copy.

"Our accountant doesn't have to handle any ledger cards any more. Any comparisons she needs to make, the computer can do for her—where she previously did it by hand or on an adding machine. By reducing the number of hand entries, it reduces the number of mistakes—and gives a much neater, cleaner, finished product."

A third major task performed by Lachman's microcomputer is inventory control. "While we don't keep a computerized perpetual inventory on all of our 10,000 different items—many of which cost less than a penny apiece—we do use the computer to keep track of certain staple, frequently used items," Cooper explains. "It keeps the records of what we purchase and sell so that we can make monthly comparisons and order more efficiently in the future."

Along with these major applications, the microcomputer also prints shipping labels when needed, prints charts, automatically types letters via a word processing program—and calculates odds for customers using Bingo and other games of chance for fund-raising purposes.

Future plans for the computer include adding payroll for

the 15-employee firm, as well as accounts receivable. "In the accounts receivable system, we plan to keep all the current accounts on line—so that the computer will be used for real-time inquiry to the data base as well as posting invoices," he points out.

"I plan to put several on-line terminals in our front office, and our billing clerks and other personnel will be able to call up any account by number, see the balance, whether it's past due, how much the customer has purchased in the past, and so on.

"The small businessman no longer has to decide, 'Do I do it by hand or spend $50,000 for a computer?'" Cooper adds. "For the cost of a bookkeeper for one year, he can pay for the whole system. Here at Lachman I can probably save one-half to one person every year because of the system. So it pays for itself in one to two years in labor savings alone."

## A PLUMBING CONTRACTOR

"That was really a stupid move, Jay. I'm going to finish you off in three moves."

Those insults are coming from Jay E. Moss' home computer, printing its barbs across a televisionlike video display screen. Moss has programmed the system to insult him as they match wits playing a four-dimensional tic-tac-toe game.

"I may make 'stupid' moves in the game, but the smartest thing I ever did was to buy that microcomputer," asserts Moss. "I got it a year ago, really as a toy for myself, but I instantly realized its potential for my plumbing contracting business.

"I've spent about $9,000 on the system in all, and I figure it has paid for itself several times over in this first year alone."

Most significantly, Moss uses the computer to develop estimates for contract bids. The system also handles various company financial activities, such as payroll and bookkeeping, and it acts as Moss' "secretary" to type out invoices and flawless form letters.

Moss' 20-year-old firm is based in Simi Valley, Cal. The

company, Jemco Plumbing Inc., does about $2.5 million in large-scale contracting annually on construction projects, mainly residential subdivisions. It employs between 20 and 40 persons, varying with the stage of construction.

About a year ago, Moss saw a news magazine article about hobbyists buying computer kits for as little as $400 and assembling small systems that are as powerful as giant computers of a decade ago.

Moss, 55, is an ardent hobbyist himself, with interests in photography, rock cutting, jewelry making, astronomy, and sailing. A mechanical engineer by training, he also has worked with electronics kits, even assembling three color TV sets. "But I knew nothing about computers beyond how to spell the word," he says.

The day after he read the article he and his son went to a computer store and spent $2,700 for an Altair 8800A microcomputer kit and peripheral equipment. Moss and his son assembled the computer over a weekend, and Moss immediately saw its business possibilities.

With the aid of the computer store personnel and an Altair basic instruction book, he developed programs for his firm's financial functions. After payroll was automated, Jemco's accountant lowered his monthly fee by $75 a month. Also, Moss uses the computer to check supplier invoices, utilizing the same system that the supplier's computer uses.

Moss also added to his system, tacking on a typewriter terminal, larger memory boards, and floppy disks for greater information-handling ability.

About six months ago, he hit on the idea of using the microcomputer to devise estimates for his contract bids. "It used to take me three to four hours with a pencil, paper, and desk calculator to estimate costs on a plan (most tracts involve three to five house plans). Now it takes me about 15 minutes at the outside," he reports.

Moss developed his own program for the computer to handle this chore. When he uses the system for estimates, it asks a series of questions: How many houses of this plan are in the tract? How many fixtures are in the plan? How much does each fixture cost? How far apart are the fixtures? How much four-inch pipe is needed for the waste system? How much three-inch pipe? Two-inch? One-and-a-half inch? In addition, there is a series of questions about the layout of the house.

The computer already knows what labor will be involved because Moss fed in records he had kept over the years of how long it takes to do each of 15 operations on a house during construction. "To check whether the computer's estimates on labor were correct, I took old housing plans from four to five years ago and had the computer estimate them. Then I checked those figures with the actual labor and costs, and they were fantastically accurate," he says.

The computer takes all the information Moss has fed into it and churns out an itemized estimate for a job, including profit and overhead factors, to produce Moss' contract bid figure. It now takes about 45 minutes to devise bids for a tract with four house plans, Moss estimates.

He adds, "Most small businessmen would probably need only about $5,500 worth of equipment. But the big thing is that they shouldn't be afraid of using a computer. They don't have to know how a computer works, only how their own business works."

# 6

# Microcomputers Provide Accounting Benefits to Small Businesses

Small businesses are just as complex as large ones, but they do not have the financial resources that large companies have to cope with accounting problems. Small businesses depend critically on the success of the sales function: order processing, inventory control, billing, and collecting. Consequently, most small businesses that acquire their own computer give primary attention to this part of their operation.

The following articles describe how various small businesses have used small computers (minicomputers or microcomputers) to obtain accounting benefits. Almost all the users quoted in these articles relate the same story: benefits that far outweigh the costs of computerization. Clerical staffs have been reduced or held even while the business has grown. Invoicing has been accelerated, improving cash flow. Aging of accounts receivable permits management to expedite collections and spot credit problems. More accurate and timely reporting of inventory status permits businesses to make better use of their capital by keeping inventories more closely aligned with sales needs. Production costs are reduced through better scheduling and materials utilization.

Small businesses today must cope with the paper flood created by greater business complexity and growing government regulations. Computerized accounting systems are helping with this problem, enabling management to concentrate on the business's real needs. Responsiveness is critical for a small business that wants to meet aggressive competition. A well-run computerized accounting system assures prompt and accurate service to customers.

This section shows how several small businesses have used the computer to help them compete with corporate giants.

## A BEER AND WINE WHOLESALER

WINE and beer, although similar in alcoholic content, are quite different when it comes to keeping track of orders and inventory.

This, combined with the increasing complexity of a business that must abide by tough state and federal regulations, prompted Kent Beverage of Grand Rapids, Mich., to seek help through purchasing a small-business system.

The firm is a beer and wine wholesaler with about 560 accounts, according to its president, Larry Gary.

"Wine is usually a presell inventory, which can be kept on the computer. The system generates a picklist and the wine is directed to the correct customer," according to Kevin Gary, general manager in charge of the small system.

Beer is a direct-sale item, so it is necessary to keep a truck inventory log overage of a consigned item. The beer salespeople make direct sales and receive cash. After the cash is brought to Kent headquarters, it is counted out manually and the resulting numbers are input into the mini via a CRT terminal. The system cost-verifies the amount and prints out a sales analysis, Gary said.

Increasing complexity in the alcoholic beverage business prompted the firm to look for a small system, the general manager said. "There are a huge number of laws wholesalers have to follow. For example, we have to keep seven years of data storage, and you can imagine the size of the data file."

Both Garys looked at several systems before choosing their present model, Kevin Gary noted. Cascade Data, Basic Four Corp., Litton, Burroughs Corp., and IBM all were contacted, and the company looked at several on-line service bureaus. "But I was not satisfied with any of the programs," Gary said.

He explained he was looking for an application package that would completely take care of his problem. The general manager had taken several computer courses in college and knew what his firm needed in a software system.

Finally, the wholesaler contacted a neighbor who happened to be a distributor for Randal Data Systems, Inc. The neighbor's firm, Minicomp Systems, Inc., was willing to write the basic programs, and Gary decided to write the rest, using his computer training. "I realized that no one really had a package for beer and wine distributors, so price dictated that we get this system," he said.

The system includes a 70 line/min. printer and floppy disk. Although one CRT is presently used on the system, Kent has another on order and has decided to switch to hard disk for more capacity. The switch requires a CPU upgrade, he noted. Initial cost was $17,000.

The firm doesn't have a hardware maintenance contract with Randal, Gary noted, because he chose to do all the maintenance himself. "The Randal equipment is as good as any other piece of hardware. Downtime has been only ¼ percent," he stated. The only problem the firm has had was a burned-out printer motor. "Service is fantastic—we get spare parts the next day."

Because the system is located in a high dust area, "I installed our own filters around the compressor," Gary noted.

He programmed the system in Randal's BASIC, which includes some variances that make the language simpler to use in writing programs, he said.

[August 1977, copyright © *Computerworld*]

## AN AUTO PARTS DISTRIBUTOR

A small business system is saving an automotive parts distributor in Hartford, Conn., between $15,000 and $25,000 annually in reduced inventory, according to the user.

The system installed at Battery Ignition Co. is also saving the firm two to eight man-hours per day in generating printed reports such as the daily operating report, lost order journal, and sales analysis by product line and part order, according to Judy Krutt, secretary and purchasing agent.

Previously on an all-manual card system, the firm decided to automate when the number of parts to keep track of reached nearly 20,000 and could no longer be handled by the old system. It looked at small systems and attended an automotive industry exposition where various systems were displayed.

"Several of the companies contacted us, but most of them could not offer local maintenance service," Krutt said. "That scared us off because availability of immediate service . . . is critical to our operations."

Battery Ignition also contacted IBM but, Krutt added, "a very important thing to us was availability of work stations. Also, we would have had to pay extra for programming because the system was not geared to our industry. Pretty soon we would have been adding dollars upon dollars to the system."

Some companies only offered hard-wired inventory systems, with the programs permanently stored in the system. "This type of system would have left us with too little flexibility," she said.

The firm finally chose a Wang Laboratories, Inc. WCS/30 system with 10M bytes of disk and a line printer. The system is connected to a Wang 2200 work station located at the front counter, and service is close by, she said.

"Before we received our Wang system in July 1976, the counter man had to go all the way from the counter to the back office to look at the card file to determine if we stocked an item. We preferred this kind of check because occasionally a line item can be in stock, yet not be immediately visible on the shelf. In this way, if the item was in stock, it was searched for until located and the sale was made," Krutt explained.

With the work station on the counter, the item can be retrieved without even interrupting telephone conversations, she noted.

The firm handles a volume of about 100 to 200 customer orders each day and the system runs full-time five and a half days each week.

The small business system has a back-order program which "allows us to keep tabs on items that our customers have ordered which we may not have in stock. We can produce a printout at the customer's request. We could never do this before. Furthermore, it makes a good impression on the customer and it's accurate."

The system also displays a warning "flag" as soon as any of the stock items drops to the reorder point. It prints the necessary reorder quantity. "Thus, warehouse space is used to maximum efficiency," she claimed.

Programs on the system generate a daily operating report; lost sales journal; sales analysis by line, location or item; low movement report; recommended order list; automatic price updates; and end of quarter and end of year reports.

[May 1977, copyright © *Computerworld*]


## A CLOTHING MANUFACTURER

A small business system user in Honolulu is finding his batch-oriented system fits his business to a "T."

That's the opinion of Radford Small, vice-president of Poly-Tees, a manufacturer of novelty T-shirts.

"With more than 1,300 customers for thousands of different T-shirt designs, colors, and sizes, we learned that a computer of our own was much more efficient and productive than trying to keep accounts by hand," Small said.

After installing an IBM 32 last fall, Poly-Tees began keeping billing and inventory information on more than 700 items, a dozen different sizes, long- and short-sleeved shirts and tie-dyed, silk-screened, air-brushed, or blank shirts.

"Before we had the computer, four clerks spent full time pricing and preparing bills," Small said.

"Now, we have three clerks and they are free for more productive work. Our customers' bills are produced quickly."

In addition to the inventory and billing functions, the system also uses data entered for those functions to product management reports—profitability analysis and sales analysis.

"Having all our business information in computer-usable form permits us to determine which items are beginning to take off in terms of demand, which are peaking out, and which ones ought to be discontinued," Small explained.

"In a business growing 75% per year, now grossing more than $3 million per year, the more control and also the more accuracy we can provide, the better able we will be to respond to the constantly changing tastes of the men, women, and children who are the ultimate customers for our shirts," he stated.

Small said Poly-Tees also markets a line of specialty perfumes which it packages and a broad range of imported goods.

The firm has a built-in bank factoring function in the system which provides the billing, inventory control, and sales analysis functions for those segments of the business, he added.

[May 1977, copyright © *Computerworld*]

## A DOOR AND WINDOW MANUFACTURER

Harcar, a manufacturer of aluminum windows, doors, bathroom enclosures and related products in Sanford, Fla., has solved a complicated order entry, inventory, and production problem by using two minicomputers.

The system, called Matrix IV, was designed by Technology Applications Laboratory (TAL) of Satellite Beach, Fla. With the two Hewlett-Packard 21MX minicomputers, Harcar can simultaneously enter a customer's order into the data base to all the business functions without reentry, according to an HP spokesman.

Other manufacturers said such a system would require a

minimum of 10 disks, but the work is being done on two, according to Carl Schilke, president of Harcar. They also said that even if it were possible, it couldn't be fully functional for nearly two years, Schilke added.

"In fact, the system is simplicity itself. Our employees are having no problems providing us with a tremendous amount of useful, detailed information," he said.

The other manufacturers also wanted to sell Harcar only packaged programs because customized programs would be too expensive. But "TAL was able to design programs for us exclusively," he said.

Previously, everything was handled manually or with the help of a calculator. In the last year and a half, however, Harcar's daily invoice mailing went from 40 to 200, and sales were expected to increase by $1 million each year for the next three years.

"I don't think we could have accommodated this kind of expansion without this system," Schilke said. "I think the paperwork would have been impossible for us to handle manually."

Harcar provides more than 50,000 options from six basic production lines with 168 standard sizes in each line. Component parts are cut from aluminum extrusions 18 to 24 feet long in mill and anodized and bronze finish.

As an order comes in, the customer's identification number is entered and an order form is displayed on a CRT showing any special shipping instructions, the customer's credit rating, the county where he is located, and the Harcar salesman in charge of the account.

The shipping dates and products ordered by their parts number are filled in by an operator. A delivery date is assigned and a delivery ticket is printed; the ticket is sent to the shipping department until the order is ready to be shipped.

All the orders of similar products scheduled for the same shipping date are pulled from the data base by the computer operator at one time in order to produce the products. In other words, the system groups all bronze windows of a certain size together, Schilke explained.

This list is checked against the finished products inventory and the system determines what products need to be manufactured. The minicomputer then goes on to break down these items into their raw material components.

The computer is also programmed to pick out the most advantageous length of extrusion and size of glass for cutting. If the best size is unavailable, the next best is selected automatically.

Information about the excess material is stored, ready to be retrieved the first time it can be used to fill an order, according to Schilke.

"This gives us tremendous raw material control," he noted. "We're able to locate the best available material quickly and use it with a minimum of waste."

After completing a production run, the system produces an efficiency report indicating the goods produced against the amount of labor required to produce them. In addition, it shows the exact costs of filling each order.

When an order is ready to be shipped, the operator calls the order form up on the CRT screen. If a back order is being filled, the operator fills in the quantity to be shipped and a back order report is prepared to indicate a completed order.

The Matrix IV system also produces management reports, including a work order report listing orders by customer and showing daily receipt of new business; buy-out reports listing items on work orders which are nonstandard and need to be purchased; reports listing sales by salesman, county, state, customer, and product; and a report listing the average discount given by product and salesman.

"With the two processors, we are achieving the kind of production and inventory control that major corporations have on a larger scale. And we are doing it with three employees who had never seen a computer in their lives until we got this system," Schilke said.

The second computer was added only recently because "we were having a problem scheduling different application work that needed to be done at the same time," according to Nina Pyle, Harcar DP manager.

[August 1977, copyright © *Computerworld*]

## A HOSPITAL SUPPLIER

Busse Hospital Disposables of Great Neck, N.Y., tossed out a paper congestion problem when it put in a turnkey minicomputer system.

Busse, a 25-year-old company with an annual volume of about $3 million in sales to the hospital market, has been using the system for more than two years.

"It took four persons to handle our business processing operations when we were doing $2 million a year, and the four were hard pressed to keep up with the volume. Today, it takes three persons to handle $3 million in sales, and nobody's working under pressure," Emanuel Cardinale, vice-president, said.

Using a manual, ledger-card-oriented NCR Corp. system, end-of-month closing for money took about a day and a half, according to Busse's system supervisor, Margaret Brumfield. With the small system, Busse has an aged trial balance within three hours of closing and is ready to go on to the following month's orders, she noted.

Inventory control is a complex matter at Busse. The product line of hospital disposables includes about 150 finished items, but the component inventory ranges into the thousands.

For example, Busse's disposable sterile tracheostomy care set is a kit comprising ten items, including the package.

Busse also has to keep track of inventory, which is consigned to converters, as well as one product line which it manufactures in a Brooklyn, N.Y. plant. Shipping takes place from Busse's warehouse in Carlstadt, N.J., and from the manufacturing plant, in some cases, drop shipments are made by converters.

Processing of orders is handled by two CRT operators. Using the STC Systems, Inc. Ultimacc Standard Distributor System, Busse makes order entry the starting point for generation of order forms and billing.

The posting of open items for customer accounts, the updating of master files, and the manipulation of information for management reports flow from the order entry procedure, Cardinale said.

Under the old system, he recalled, three persons were involved in preparing orders for one machine operator. First, the customer ledger card was pulled and the order attached; the order then went to the bookkeeper for a credit check.

After the order was returned for pricing and inventory control, the invoice was run through the machine. One of the clerks then had to type shipping labels and bills of lading, fill in the weight of the shipment, and recalculate the billing extensions to make sure no errors had been made.

The ledger card system had been purchased three years earlier. "We thought it would meet our needs for six or seven years, but as our volume grew the system became less and less functional," Cardinale said.

Credit checking, another important benefit for Busse, helps keep track of the current status of 1,500 customers. "We never had an aged trial balance with our old system. Therefore, an inactive account could remain unpaid for a long time without necessarily attracting our attention.

"Of course, a new order would stimulate a demand for payment, but we couldn't rely on that to keep current. With Ultimacc, we have a much better handle on receivables," Cardinale said.

The decision to acquire a minicomputer-based system was slow in coming. "The small businessman doesn't think in terms of a computer to solve this type of problem. Most of us believe computer systems are too sophisticated for such matters and far too expensive," Cardinale explained.

After being solicited by a sales representative and after seeing a system in operation at a business of similar size on Long Island, Busse hired a consultant to consider minis from STC, IBM, Basic/Four, and NCR. "With our consultant's help, we decided that Ultimacc was most appropriate for our needs," Cardinale said.

[October 1977, copyright © *Computerworld*]

## A LUMBER DISTRIBUTOR

A turnkey minicomputer at a wholesale distributor to the lumber business in Dallas has coped with this company's increased growth, according to a spokesman.

"In the last year [before installing the system] we have almost doubled our business, and it was either go to a computer or hire additional clerks to sit at additional typewriters and bookkeeping machines," Steve Baker, accounting manager for Dallas Wholesale Builders Supply, Inc. said.

The company has sales in excess of $1 million/mo. of materials such as panels, moldings, and doors. It has about 500 customers ranging in location from the Gulf of Mexico to Oklahoma, he added.

The firm made the decision to look for a minicomputer because Baker felt a small system would fit the size of the business. A minicomputer also "offered a lot more to us than a batch system associated with larger scale computers," Baker said. A real-time environment was a must, he noted.

The primary applications the company needed on the system immediately were billing and inventory, so the firm searched for a system suited to its needs. Finally, a turnkey mini dealer with systems in the wholesale distributor's area came to the company's attention.

"The software it had at that point in time was basically what we needed, with some enhancements in some areas," he said. In addition, the Data General Corp. (DG) hardware used in the Electrofile, Inc. configuration seemed to be a good choice.

The system was installed as a complete turnkey from Electrofile. It includes a 32K-word DG Nova, disk, a teletypewriter, three CRTs, and two printers. One of the printers, an 80 char./sec. model, is used exclusively to produce delivery tickets. All the programs are written in FORTRAN running under DG's Disk Operating System, he added.

Prior to acquiring the automated system, the firm had been using an Olivetti bookkeeping machine, he continued.

The system now handles receivables, payables, inventory,

purchasing, historical sales reports, and order entry. The company has about seven inside and seven outside salespeople and, when orders are taken, they code an order sheet, from which the orders are then entered into the system. The historical sales data presents management information such as the percentage of profits and breaks the information down by salesperson.

The installation was up and running with invoicing and billing within a month after the computer was installed, he continued. This was a big factor in its choice, since the crunch of added sales was bogging down the firm's turnaround time.

All the system components are known manufacturers' equipment, he said, so the risks in deciding on a turnkey system were minimized. The company also "checked the background" of the turnkey house before the purchase to assure it was a solid company, Baker noted.

[August 1976, copyright © *Computerworld*]

## A HOUSE-PLANT DISTRIBUTOR

The minicomputer at Hickerson Flowers in Apopka, Fla., has solved the firm's "paper blizzard problem" and allowed business to grow at an increased rate, according to the company's general manager.

Prior to automating, Hickerson, a wholesale dealer of Florida-grown house plants, had been using an NCR accounting machine for invoicing and monthly reports, Lillian O'Connell said.

When the company decided more in-house power was needed, the firm considered minicomputers from IBM, Burroughs, NCR, and Digital Equipment Corp. (DEC). The DEC system was chosen because "we felt it was designed to do the job better than the others and came highly recommended from people who had the system," O'Connell said.

The system, a Datasystem 340 with 32K bytes of memory, was customized for the foliage industry by Parcomp, Inc., a Cocoa, Fla., OEM software house. The configuration includes

6M bytes of disk, three CRTs, a Decwriter, and a 300 line/min. printer; it cost the firm about $60,000.

Before the installation of the system about a year ago, the order entry process was strictly manual. Routing lists, delivery tickets, redelivery lists, shipping labels and bills of lading were hand-typed. Extra part-time help was needed to generate the documents for large orders.

Three former clerk/typists now handle the order entry system. The system routes orders to their destinations and keeps a running inventory of plants that are maturing and ready to be shipped, O'Connell said.

The error rate for shipments has been reduced, she added. Shipments are routed, addressed, and priced more accurately, and there is an automatic pricing structure built into the system with a special price override capability, she said.

With the system, all documents needed for filling a 3,200-case order, excluding invoices, have been generated within four hours, she noted, including time for data entry.

[August 1976, copyright © *Computerworld*]

## AN ACCOUNTING FIRM

Better control, tighter security, and faster turnaround—those are the reasons many users give for switching from a service bureau to an in-house system.

The Wellesley, Mass., office of LaFrance, Walker, Jackley and Saville here is one such user, according to the partners in charge.

Small to medium-size manufacturing, trading, and other concerns comprise the main portion of the CPA's client base.

When asked why a small firm of certified public accountants (CPA) would consider an in-house computer, Charles Morse, one of the partners, explained, "Our primary reason was to improve turnaround time on clients' information."

The principal workload of the firm is general ledger and financial statement preparation. Information is input from footed journals, which are totals from the clients' various journals. This input is then used to prepare the general ledger and, as a by-product, a financial statement.

Time is often a critical factor in this operation, according to Morse. "Sometimes governmental agencies, banks, lending institutions, or boards of directors have very critical time deadlines by which they must see information.

"Security is also very important," he added. "We do not like client information leaving the office."

During a typical working day, a member of the firm travels to a client's premises and meets with the client's bookkeeper or clerk who has prepared posting journals from the books of original entry.

Several hours are spent checking that information and preparing corrected or updated entries. The results are then brought to the accounting office, where the general ledger and financial statements are updated and completed.

"Before we purchased our Wang Laboratories, Inc. system, we relied on an outside service bureau for general ledger and financial statement preparation," Morse said.

"We were using an optical font adding machine at our office," he continued. "This produced computer-recognizable numbers which were scanned optically at the center. These were then converted to magnetic tape, which was sent through the computer.

"This process typically involved a five- or six-day waiting period, just to get our information returned. Sometimes we received information back and found we had to make a change either because of a client error, our error, a service bureau error, or because the computer made a mistake."

The CPA firm went in-house also because "we felt in the long run we would realize a dollar saving," Morse said. "The cost of the outside service bureau would be approximately equal to what we would be spending to amortize our own system."

Now when a client's information is brought to the firm on a series of posting journals, it is input into one of the floppy disks of the Wang WCS-20 system. That information is then integrated into the previous history record (which was stored on the client's disk) and an updated history record is produced.

The system then runs off financial statements, such as a balance sheet or income statements.

[October 1977, copyright © *Computerworld.*]

## A MICROCOMPUTER SUPPLIER FOR MEDICAL OFFICES

Promedics Data Corp. of Palo Alto, Cal., has introduced a turnkey microcomputer system for accounting applications in medical offices that incorporates a hobby microcomputer and standard peripherals.

The PAC 1 is an 8080-based system that uses the S-100 design and incorporates dual Shugart Associates floppy disk drives, a Digital Equipment Corp. LA-36 hard-copy printer, and a Perkin-Elmer Fox CRT. The turnkey system uses Promedics applications software.

The system allows a doctor or small clinic to establish uniform accounting procedures for patient ledgers and gives random access to patient information seconds after the account is keyed in, according to a spokesman. A special report generator allows each end user to configure individual reports using any information stored in the patient data base, he added.

The current PAC 1 uses two 16K dynamic memory boards, a dual serial I/O board, and either a Z80 or 8080 MPU card. An additional disk interface card is also housed in the system, he said.

Complementing the hardware is a disk operating system and language compiler/interpreter that generates a pseudo-operating code which can be run independently from the source code.

The disk operating system takes up approximately 20K bytes of memory, leaving 12K for application and data, the spokesman noted. Larger programs can be implemented by either adding more memory or using the operating system's overlay capabilities, he claimed.

Promedics has found the hobby-type computer mainframe to be reliable and cost-effective when built and tested to commercial standards, he said. The firm is committed to microcomputers and believes "hobby computers are here to stay if they can be used for practical DP applications and achieve a price/performance ratio lower than their competition," he stated.

A PAC 1 system costs $13,500, which includes operator training and support for one year.

[September 1977, copyright © *Computerworld*]

## A RETAIL SUPPLIES MANUFACTURER

A turnkey small business system at ABC Hanger and Supply, Inc. in Garden City, N.Y., has helped this firm gain control over its accounts receivable and inventory, according to Howard Schulman, vice-president.

The firm, which furnishes ready-to-wear retailers with supplies ranging from hangers to wrapping aids, ships and receives its orders through the mail.

Until April 1976, the $2.5 million company struggled through invoicing with one Friden and one Hermes billing machine. At that time the firm was invoicing customers two and a half weeks after the merchandise was shipped. The merchandise went out on time, but not the invoice, Shulman noted.

Seeking a better alternative, Schulman opted for an IBM System 32, expecting that order entry, accounts receivable, and invoicing could be speeded and customer service improved. He hoped to automate inventory as well.

Schulman accepted the System 32 with a 3741 data input station and the accompanying MNAS program. The company was never able to get past order entry and invoicing in nine months with the customized package purchased from IBM.

Schulman hired two extra people who spent every morning assigning account numbers. They punched numbers in, but if nonvalid numbers were entered, they did not find out and merchandise was shipped to the wrong customer. As a result, extra people had to be hired to edit the already entered orders, he added.

By September 1976, Schulman had had enough and looked for a better way. He saw just about every minicomputer manufacturer's system, including Basic Four Corp., Nixdorf, Digital Equipment Corp. and Burroughs. A total responsibility "turnkey" system was the objective, Schulman said.

In November 1976, ABC was contacted by Turnkey Sales & Leasing, Inc., a New York City-based distributor of minicomputer systems. Schulman visited two user installations, saw a demonstration, and made the decision to switch. The turnkey house evaluated the company's needs and recommended the Microdata Corp. Reality system.

"Even though their price was $10,000 higher than the other systems, we felt it was worth it," Schulman reported.

"Interactivity, immediate real-time response, ability to do whatever we wanted, whenever we wanted it done, was important in the selection," he noted. "Turnkey's approach of providing a system on a customer requirement basis, the use of English, and the versatility in extracting information from the system were the things that impressed me," Schulman stated. "Turnkey didn't try to put me into the computer business," he added.

Shulman ordered the Microdata Reality system from Turnkey on November 15, 1976. The system was delivered on schedule, February 9, 1977. In six days, the entire system was operational. After one week, the system processed 1,400 orders and billed 1,000 customers in 10 days.

Sales analysis enables ABC to prepare its catalogs based on which items are selling. Invoices are in the mail the day after shipment so the customer can verify the items and quantities he ordered and know when and how his order was shipped. Cash flow has improved and credit checks are accurate, Schulman said.

The system also segregates custom items from drop-ship items and warehoused items and will create purchase orders to suppliers of the "specials." Stock items are put on a picking list.

Also, with certain items which are not warehoused on a regular basis, but brought in for shipment, the system recognizes these items, prints them on a picking order, and creates a purchase order for vendors with instructions to ship them into ABC's warehouse.

The system also accommodates quantity price differentials and is able to price out any item. The system maintains price breaks as they relate to quantity and posts the right price.

Another important facet is the handling of multi-item, prepaid orders. The amount of the payment is carried in an order file. Cash is applied to the first shipment.

For example, if a prepaid order for $100 is received and the first shipment is invoiced for $50, the system issues an itemized paid invoice which totals $50 and details $50 credit remaining on the account. If the second shipment is for another $50, the system again issues an itemized paid invoice and states "zero balance." If the second shipment exceeds the outstanding balance (e.g., a $70 shipment), the system issues a paid invoice of $50 with a "balance due" of $20. Account statements are issued at the end of each month.

[August 1977, copyright © *Computerworld*]

## AN AIR FREIGHT COMPANY

A good alternative approach to a first computer system is the do-it-yourself approach. For the company that doesn't have an existing EDP staff, and doesn't want to go the turnkey route, the new easy-to-use hardware and software enable non-technical employees to master data processing principles quickly and easily. The result can be low-cost systems with full management control over the operation.

Intercontinental Air Freight, Inc., is an import/export service based at Boston's Logan International Airport. The company arranges shipments between six continents on 100 cargo-carrying world airlines and has offices in London, Paris, and Frankfurt. It's a financially complex business dealing with a variety of customs fees, currencies, and rates of foreign exchange—plus all standard business accounting such as invoicing, billing, and disbursements. After 10 years in operation, the company faced a decision to do one of two things: add more people or computerize.

Robert Maloney, Intercontinental's president, believes that success in business depends on keeping costs down, exercising full control over operations, and holding labor to a minimum staff of congenial, loyal employees with a good understanding of the business.

When Intercontinental first considered data processing, its initial step was to use a service bureau. The company manually gathered accounting documents and sent them to the service bureau for processing. But this had drawbacks. Documents were sometimes lost. Data was processed monthly with a five-day turnaround time—longer if errors occurred. The result was a substantial lack of control, late billing, and sluggish cash flow.

The answer for Intercontinental seemed to be an in-house computer. Early in the planning stages, management made a basic decision to avoid interim measures such as buying an accounting machine or a prepackaged system. This decision was based on anticipated increase in the workload and appreciation of the growth potential offered by a computer system.

"It took a considerable amount of time to learn how to talk to computer vendors and to acquire the basic knowledge required to evaluate hardware and software," said Maloney. "In the process, we came close to making some mistakes." Maloney was about to buy a batch system when he learned of the transaction-oriented on-line method of processing. After a thorough comparison, the transaction-oriented method seemed to fit Intercontinental's business structure better, and Maloney decided to purchase a DEC Datasystem 340 from Digital Equipment Corporation. Costs were low, and the core expandability, ease of programming, and in-house control fit Intercontinental's needs perfectly.

Management decided to train in-house employees to program and operate the system. Although this would require more time than adopting a turnkey system, it had two major advantages: it was less expensive than hiring a new staff whose only function was data processing, and it would ensure that the systems—being developed by long-time employees who thoroughly understood the business—fit like a glove. Changes, which occur with time, could be implemented as quickly as management needed them.

Software for the system was a successful pioneer effort by specialist Eric Levine, now president of Business Systems Research of North Andover, Mass. Levine spent three weeks with Intercontinental's accounting department learning the import/export business.

Meanwhile, Maloney sent one of his employees, Roger O. Paquin, to attend Digital's two-week programming school for an introduction to computers and to learn DIBOL (Digital Business Oriented Language). By the time Levine had a grasp of the Intercontinental operation, Paquin had learned enough about computers so that the two could communicate with one another. That solved Intercontinental's most troublesome problem and resulted in successful programs that suited the company's needs.

Since that time, Paquin and several others have taken advantage of other courses at the Digital training center. Reinforced with three semesters of data processing courses at Northeastern University, Paquin not only modifies and maintains the original software but is capable of working up any specialized programs that management requires.

The Datasystem 340 consists of a PDP-8/E minicomputer with 16K of memory and can store 3.2 million characters on two disk drives. Combined with the software, it forms a self-contained system that provides analyses and reports necessary to make intelligent management decisions. It operates in a direct data processing mode, dedicated to the single task of data editing or document printing. The operator interacts with the computer by entering transaction data in a pre-defined format through a keyboard/CRT. This data can then be verified against files, so that errors are discovered and corrected while the source document is still available to the operator.

One of the first systems installed handles all import calculations. It stores almost the entire book of tariffs of the U.S. Customs Office on line—10,000 items. Every category of goods has a four-digit identification number. When this number is entered into the computer, the system applies the proper rate of duty, prints a description of the goods, including all values required by customers, adds up the total sum owed, and commands the printer to put out the information on the required forms in multiples of nine. An entry card summarizing the shipment, specifying the importer of record and other customs details, is tagged on at the bottom.

At the end of the month, the computer yields summary reports on how much freight Intercontinental has handled; who is doing most of the shipping; and financial reports on total sales, payments to customs, outstanding bills. In the course of any one month, the firm lays out up to $3 million on behalf of its clients. With this large amount of money involved, steady cash flow is a must. The company makes it clear to its customers that immediate payment is necessary so the money is there to put to work for them again.

Intercontinental also uses the computer to arrange letters of credit, along with specialized services such as consular invoices, drafts, export declarations, etc. Charges for these services must be picked up along the line. The computer keeps a running tally, so that Intercontinental has up-to-date records of all charges, who has paid, and what is owed. This keeps the books cleared within 20 days, according to Maloney.

Time savings? Considerable. For example, accounts receivable information—due every two weeks—is extracted in a matter of minutes. Done manually, this used to require three days.

Intercontinental is converting to a DEC Datasystem 356, a larger system based on the PDP-11/40 central processor.

Their ambitious systems program now has the capability to handle all export documentation on line, generate airline billings automatically, produce reporting for the Civil Aeronautics Board, handle temporary import bonds, and is growing constantly. Says Maloney: "The system not only paid for itself in savings in time and labor; it made it possible for us to handle business we could not have handled otherwise."

[*Modern Office Procedures*, October 1976, copyright © Penton/IPC, subsidiary of Pittway Corporation]

## AN AIR POLLUTION FILTRATION MANUFACTURER

The installation of a small business system has helped Steelcraft Corp. of Memphis, Tenn., cope with a swelling customer base and the resulting paperwork blizzard, according to assistant treasurer D.A. Drewes.

The company manufactures pneumatic dust-handling systems for the woodworking, grain, and paper industries and also produces motor bases and angle rings.

"As the customer base grew to well over 1,000, paperwork also grew. With assorted price lists, the hand-invoicing became too error-prone and the hand-posting too laborious to tolerate," he explained.

To remedy the situation, the Wang Laboratories, Inc. 2200 minicomputer was selected in May of 1974 and program installation began that August. Since acquisition of the minicomputer, the firm has installed a receivable, payable, and payroll system, which includes product line and salesmen's sales analyses as side benefits of the invoicing programs.

In addition, the invoice files are scanned for specific product sales to provide production control, and, together with the necessary sales data, reports are produced that forecast future needs. From the master customer files also come monthly statements and collection letters.

After the basic systems were operational, the company added several applications. Initial applications were programmed by the software dealer, but Drewes did the rest himself.

Asset and depreciation listings were computerized and annual depreciation charges were calculated. This eliminated burdensome lap schedules. In addition, shop equipment maintenance records were stored on disk and maintenance requests were automatically generated at the proper intervals.

Mailing list programs were also written which could access either the customer master file or purchased lists and then output the proper letter. Price and weight sheets of various standard manufactured items were kept up to date and provided to sales personnel as required. Time cards were printed from payroll records, along with lists by seniority and birthdate as well as lists required for various pension and profit-sharing plans. The firm also designed programs which provide sales and sales tax by state for required government tax reports.

Currently two systems to aid the manufacturing division are under development. The first is for use with recently purchased numerically controlled punch and cutting equipment. The program generates the necessary coordinates to cut flat patterns for elbow gores.

This is a mathematical program utilizing trigonometric functions and layout procedures developed over the years for sheet metal products.

The other system under way will aid in order control, production, and erection scheduling. The first portion consists of a field erection schedule, which divides the job into various systems required and traces the progress from original scheduled performance through actual costs of erection. It also tracks the ahead or behind condition through field analyses of percentages of completion.

If more than one system is tied together for erection purposes, the schedule will adjust to this situation as progress is charted. The total schedule will provide quick data on whether the target completion will be met or will indicate that steps must be taken to correct the situation.

The program involved will handle any job with 40 or

fewer divisions. Actually, the number 40 is controlled by the 132-column print capability of the high-speed printer, since each division requires three columns plus room on the left of the form for date information.

[August 1977, copyright © *Computerworld*]

## A FARMING COOPERATIVE

Trying to communicate ideas and solutions through systems people and programmers to a computer was a difficult but necessary task until my firm, New Cooperative, Inc. of Vincent, Iowa, got its portable small business system.

When IBM came out with the 5100 portable system about a year and a half ago, I was convinced this was my opportunity to learn the BASIC language and write programs to get the results I wanted.

New Cooperative is a farm cooperative located in a small town. The business is larger than an average-size company and sales this year will be about $36 million.

Cooperatives face a unique accounting problem. All transactions of the member/owners have to be maintained so that dividends can be distributed based on their patronage.

After receiving the 5100 it took seven months to write and debug the necessary programs. Presently we are running 65 programs on the system, 17 of which pertain to the patronage and members' equity problem. We can write payroll checks to 50 employees in one hour and mail 1,300 monthly statements to patrons on the second work day of the month.

Customer statements are itemized in the language familiar to the customer so, for example, corn sales to the company is Corn Purchases to the customer.

The system also provides management with departmental preliminary profit and loss and balance sheets on the second work day of a month. The general ledger trial balance is also run on the first work day of each month.

Sales analysis and budget creation are two more key applications for the unit. In the budget applications the company uses the portable system in the conference room to directly input the departmental budgets and then print out results. Revisions made to the budgets during the year are easily incorporated.

Accounts receivable aging can be listed any time during the month. In addition, the system computes and writes checks to the member/owners showing a detailed history of their equity holdings in the cooperative. It also provides listings of warehouse receipts held by the customer either in alphabetical order or by number. Checks can be sorted on the system and listed in numerical order for easier bank reconciliation.

All of these applications plus the convenience of a computer that is simple enough for me and my three employees to operate has made me realize there are advantages to in-house computing. I learned how to program from the manuals that came with the computer.

The cost of the system was also very attractive. The basic system cost about $25,000. The software was written in-house. The maintenance agreement is $110/mo. Paper cost is about $25/mo. Total monthly cost, not including investment credit, using straight-line five-year depreciation is $555.

The cost of the previous system, which was a CRT connected to a service center 500 miles away, was between $1,100 and $1,300/mo.

This is a savings of $650/mo., with no increase in personnel. The best thing is now we have a "feel" for the accounting we do because we do it all in house.

[August 1977, copyright © *Computerworld*]


## A COUNTY GOVERNMENT

Pottawattamie County pulled its payroll off a service bureau and its accounting applications off an outdated accounting machine and put them on two minicomputers to save time and improve work flow.

The county DP center in Council Bluffs, Iowa, decided to

purchase the Olivetti A5 minicomputers more than a year ago, and the county auditor, Douglas Primmer, feels it's the best choice that could have been made. "Expense-wise, it's the best—we have two machines for the price of one," he explained.

Primmer looked at Burroughs and NCR equipment as well as the A5, but decided that for the county's needs the simpler system seemed the best, he said.

The county's problem wasn't really speed but workflow, he recalled. "We were working with slow turnaround time and an antiquated system," he said.

In addition, the payroll for the more than 400 county employees was done by an outside vendor and the turnaround time was not good, according to Primmer.

When an error occurred on a payroll check, it could not be corrected until the next paycheck was issued. Now an error can be corrected immediately.

Now, one minicomputer performs payroll and checkwriting applications and the other handles the accounting functions. In addition, one A5 is used for program development; the other runs the applications.

In case of a pinch, Primmer said, both could be used for one function; if one went down, the other could be used as a backup. The systems also perform all the bookkeeping and produce reports for the county, which has a population of 90,000.

In addition to providing faster turnaround time, the systems are easier to use and the number of operator errors have therefore been reduced, Primmer said.

Olivetti has provided good service and maintenance since the sale, he said, adding the vendor maintains all the county's data on cards which can be used on Olivetti's own system, if necessary.

The county's A5 systems might be expanded if the work keeps increasing and it proves necessary, Primmer commented.

Pottawattamie's present systems are valued at about $16,850, including programming and maintenance. The basic components of each system include a microprocessor, random-access memory, keyboard, printer, magnetic card unit, communications logic, and logic to accommodate optional peripheral devices.

[October 1977, copyright © *Computerworld*]

## A CITY GOVERNMENT

Aspen, probably best known for its extensive ski areas, is a small Colorado city with a permanent population under 10,000 and an annual municipal budget currently about $7.5 million. Despite its size, the city government is active. Aspen, like most other cities, operates water, electrical, and transportation utilities in addition to school, police, fire, and other services.

Since 1971 Aspen has used a small computer to automate its accounting functions. The original incentives for the data processing move were to reduce labor intensity, save time, and ensure accuracy in water and electricity billing, payroll processing, and general ledger accounting. The first installation used a payroll package, a series of accounting programs from the city's auditing firm, and utility billing software, developed within the city finance department.

After only two years, however, Aspen had outgrown this system. More than 60 programs were routinely run and the number of records being processed had almost reached maximum computer capacity. Although already experiencing delays, especially during month-end tabulating periods, the finance department was asking for new and expanded applications.

To help solve this problem, the city hired Bruce Anderson and Scott Keller, consultants, Snowmass Systems. Their task included increasing the utilization of the existing equipment by revising inefficient programs, eliminating apparent problem areas, and adding several new features and functions. Snowmass Systems was also asked to help participate in a study to determine if a new or upgraded DP center would be feasible.

To guide investigations of new equipment, a number of criteria were established. Economic constraints were particularly severe; the cost of hardware ownership was not to exceed the $1,700 monthly already being allocated for DP equipment and the total operating costs were to be under the $2,000 per month then being spent. To avoid conversion problems, the new equipment would have to support a version of the RPG language compatible with that in the original programs. Since downtime would be critical, all hardware was to be available from a single source and be fully supported. Maintenance contracts would be necessary with dependable service from an office in Denver. The city recognized that many of its applications were specialized, so some program development would be needed; however, the configuration purchased would have to support commercial tasks, including sophisticated file management, to provide tools for software creation and modification as well as efficient operation.

Cost, in this tall order, was the most difficult criterion to meet. In most cases, the difference was a factor of three or more, which obviated even looking for alternative justification opportunities. The closest match to Aspen's requirements was the Data General Eclipse C/300. In the configuration necessary for the application, the purchase price would, following standard city accounting practices, represent about $2,700 per month.

Since the minimal C/300 configuration needed to support municipal requirements had greater speed and memory access capacity than the city could utilize, an opportunity for economy existed if slight expansion could accommodate one or more additional users. The government of surrounding Pitkin County expressed an interest in sharing DP facilities. This was particularly attractive because many of the applications were similar and because the county office building was directly across the street from city hall. Moreover, a system that would meet the needs of both governments could be purchased for an additional $10,000, so the total facility would cost each user about $1,500 per month.

The initial hardware configuration included 128K bytes of core memory, two 10M byte disks of mass memory, a 300 lpm printer, a magnetic tape drive, a CRT operator console, and four CRT user terminals—two in each building. Software included the Data General INFOS file management system with an RPG-II compiler for programming.

The benefits of the extra capacity were apparent immediately. The older equipment required between 8 and 14 hours to produce the month-end general ledger and no other work could be done during this period. The new system produces the general ledger in two hours and can, simultaneously, handle multiple users. In addition to speed, accounting accuracy has improved and specialized reports can be obtained routinely or upon request without overloading the system.

[*Infosystems,* August 1977, copyright © Hitchcock Publishing Co.]

## A BEER DISTRIBUTOR

When a beer distributor in Dover, N.J., decided it was time to add a new line of brew, it turned to a minicomputer to deal with the expected volume of paperwork.

As a result of the installation of the small system, the firm reduced errors, cut the time it takes to route trucks, and substantially improved its collections procedures.

About two years ago, American Corp. bought out half of another beer distributor to gain the Schlitz/Ballantine portion of the distributorship, according to Alan Chernotsky, owner of the firm. "With the increased business we expected from the new line, we just didn't feel we could handle the increased paperwork," Chernotsky said. "We had 425 customers two years ago; now we service 750."

According to Chernotsky, the increase in business would have been too much for his 22 employees, who include drivers, warehousemen, and clerical support. "I knew we needed some kind of automatic processing," he said. "We looked at striped ledger systems and mechanical bookkeeping machines, but they didn't do half the job we needed done.

"Then we looked at computers. I guess we must have looked at 10 different kinds. Most of them didn't have much software, and the ones that did had canned software packages which the companies refused to modify."

Chernotsky said he first heard about his present system, a Wang Laboratories, Inc. WCS-30, through an advertisement. When he investigated, he found that while no software existed for beer distributors, a system performing inventory, invoicing, and cash receipts operations similar to what he needed was installed at a nearby fuel oil dealer.

"To me, this was a good example of the kind of system I had been looking for," he noted. "Everyone else I talked to said their systems did these operations perfectly, but nobody could show me any installations."

Confident that the system could handle the increased paperwork, Chernotsky decided to purchase it before he added Schlitz and Ballantine.

"I wanted to have our system up and running beforehand," he said. "I didn't want to be in the position of converting all our records over to the system at the same time we were trying to add a new line. That would have been absolute chaos."

Contracting with a programmer, Chernotsky was able to develop programs defined to his requirements and tailored to his needs.

His list of applications includes order entry for new sales; route assignment for his 11 trucks; a daily sales journal and summary; daily cash receipts; an inventory report, including a value report; an aged accounts receivable, payroll, and accounts payable; and a sales analysis by salesman, customer, or product.

The system also delivers complete accounting functions from cash disbursements to general ledger and all journals.

Chernotsky knew he would have to transfer all of his files from his manual system to the computer; during the process, he had to run duplicate files for two months. But he turned the situation to his advantage, he said, by updating all customer files as they were entered into the system.

"My salesmen made up slips for each customer to get records up to date. Now I won't let a file get out of date, and I have my operators make any changes on the spot." he added.

Because errors are reduced, the firm no longer wastes manpower and postage sending corrections to customers. Truck routing that used to take four people all day can now be accomplished by one operator in under two hours.

The largest advantage Chernotsky reported was improved collections. "Because my system provides accurate aged balances, I know immediately all receivables over 30 days and I have increased collections substantially.

"Also, the New Jersey Alcoholic Beverage Commission requires a statement of all customers with billings over 30 days, and now I can print it out daily without any hassles," he added.

[*Computerworld*, February 1978, copyright © CW Communications/Inc.]


## A MARINE SUPPLIER

Tired of "borrowing" time on an IBM 3/10 from a friend on nights and weekends, Jeremy Crews, president of Marine Development Corp. of Richmond, Va., decided to go in house with a GRI-99 minicomputer.

"I got started on the IBM 3/10 about four years ago," Crews explained, "when we got into a real bind. Our annual sales were $2 million and we found ourselves with $1 million in parts inventory," he said.

"We couldn't get our billings out fast enough and we couldn't ship because we couldn't get parts," the manufacturer of boat air-conditioning systems noted.

"Purchasing couldn't get parts because we hadn't paid our supplier's bills; accounting couldn't pay the bills because we had borrowed to the extent of our credit line to pay for our $1 million worth of parts on hand."

Crews began to design a manual, parts-forecast system.

After it took three people four hours to develop a usage forecast for the first of 3,500 detail parts for the company's 600 products, he decided to seek an automated solution to the inventory trouble.

To try to bring the situation under control, Crews "borrowed" time on an IBM 3/10 from a friend and learned how to program the system himself. His friend didn't want just anybody from the company using the system, he explained, so he did all the work.

The effort was successful, he reported. For the first time the company knew the number of products each detail part was used to build, the number of parts on hand, and how many parts should be purchased on what date to meet the production schedule.

"I got tired of nights and weekends and decided to look for an in-house system," Crews said. The company examined several systems, including the 3/10, which it dismissed as too expensive; the IBM 32; Burroughs B700; systems from NCR; Basic Four; and Logical Machines Corp.'s Adam system. He chose the GRI-99 because it came closest to having the flexibility and capability of the IBM 3/10 at "the right kind of price."

Another reason the company switched to the GRI machine is that it is cardless and "we didn't want to fool with cards anymore." Input on the GRI system is via CRT terminals, he noted.

The firm purchased the GRI-99 about a year ago from Automated Data Systems, the local GRI distributor, which also provides service for the system. Crews described the service as good.

The configuration includes a 24-byte CPU, disk drive, two CRT terminals, and a 100 line/min. printer. To expand the current system, the firm has ordered a third CRT terminal, a second printer, and an additional 8K bytes of main memory.

Conversion to the system was straightforward; card files were transferred to disk storage. Because the local GRI distributor owns a duplicate model of the computer, the company was able to begin conversion even before its system 99 was delivered.

The firm's system now handles payroll, shipping orders, invoices, accounts payable, accounts receivable, vendor files, dealer files, cross-reference information, back orders, and an overseas subsidiary's records, in addition to materials control.

"Our sales are twice what they were four years ago, but our inventory is down from $1 million to $400,000. Now we only stock the parts we need and we ship finished products on time," Crews said.

"I really appreciate the flexibility of this machine. We can set up files and reports just about any way we want. We can change programs and recompile right on the machine in just a few minutes. We can even set up a series of reports to run on an or/if basis so that the computer can decide which program should be run next without anyone being there to tell it. There are all kinds of things we can do," he said.

"I'm really convinced it's the best machine I could get for the money," Crews stated.

[August 1977, copyright © *Computerworld*]

## AN AUTO PARTS MANUFACTURER

A small business system at a unique division of a Fortune 500 company in Churubusco, Ind., is helping the division gain control over its dedicated application.

The company, Dana Corp., is a $1.5 billion firm based in Toledo, Ohio. Its automotive marketing division is heavily involved in the replacement parts business and the cataloging application that inevitably goes with that business.

In the mid-1950s, the firm decided the catalog task had outgrown conventional methods, according to Frank Sedlacek, manager of cataloging systems.

Catalog methods have to be timely, accurate and all-inclusive, he said, noting catalogs are drawn from voluminous numerical and constantly changing data.

Sedlacek considered a computer ideally suited for catalog preparation based upon his experience with automation in typesetting applications.

With persistence, he was able to secure time on Dana's central mainframe. Until recently, he continued to use the help of the company's mainframe on a time-sharing batch process basis.

As his cataloging tasks continued to grow, time on the mainframe became harder to get for tasks like his, and batch processing became less acceptable to him. His parts cataloging requirements soon outgrew their welcome on the mainframe.

Each year's new car models add to the volume of parts information that must be managed and presented. "The parts business increases at a fast rate; newer models are introduced faster than older models are retired," he noted.

Dana, he said, must completely revise and publish 12 master catalogs every two years and supply supplemental catalogs during the interim period.

The next step for Dana was a switch to a Linolex Systems Co., Inc. small business system that was adequate for its needs at the time. When more power was needed, the firm looked at systems from IBM and Microdata Corp.; it chose a Microdata because "you couldn't beat the price." That was three years ago.

Systems Management, Inc., a Microdata dealer, recommended a system that consists of a CPU with 20M bytes of disk storage, a 9-track 800 bit/in. magnetic tape drive, two CRT terminals and a 96 char./sec. printer. The printer provides both upper and lower case characters.

Two drives, four terminals, and 16K of memory have since been added to the system.

The system was installed in the Automotive Division's Toledo facility in November 1975. When the division was moved to Churubusco, the system went right along "without a slip," according to Sedlacek.

With its Reality system, Sedlacek said, the division was able to produce its "Victor" catalog without overtime for the first time. Victor is a Dana brand name, and Sedlacek noted that publication of the previous Victor catalog had cost 1,150 man-hours of overtime, or $15,000 in out-of-pocket expenses.

Furthermore, Sedlacek added, the catalog was published

with a completely new format. He believed that making this format change without the system's help would have cost approximately $3,200 for keypunching and $2,100 for purchased time. The system saved $20,300 on this publication alone, he estimated.

Savings were also achieved with the system's elimination of the input and proofreading time previously required.

"The system paid for itself within a year," Sedlacek noted.

Sedlacek found he could produce a price list in five working days and "get it out about 10 days earlier." This, he said, allowed the firm to advance the effective data by two weeks.

The system also enabled the division to streamline its manufacturing process. Duplicate parts were identified and have since been eliminated along with the cost of duplicate listing, pricing, and warehousing. "This updating has become a continuous cost-saving process," Sedlacek said.

The firm is able to link publications, sales, source, and engineering records into one integrated file.

[*Computerworld*, January 1978, copyright © CW Communications/Inc.]

# 7

# Microcomputers Help Small Businesses Manage and Produce Revenues

The value of small computers for business is not limited to accounting functions. Many small businesses are using these inexpensive but powerful machines to assist in operating management and in some cases to generate revenue.

Engineering and architectural companies regularly use computers to assist in designing buildings, plants, and refineries. Broadcasting stations and cable TV systems use computers to schedule programs, control studio operation, and analyze advertising effectiveness. Banks, insurance companies, and mortgage companies use computers to prepare legal and financial documents. Shipping companies use computers for dispatching and transportation control, cost analysis, and legal compliance. Brokerage houses use small computers for trading, order placement, and underwritings in addition to customer accounting.

*The following articles illustrate how small businesses use minicomputers and microcomputers in ways that go beyond, but often include, accounting functions.*

## A REAL ESTATE INVESTMENT FIRM

"Basically, . . . we're controlling the financial reporting of the company," says James A. Sorensen, vice president, financial department, Urban Investment and Development Co., Chicago, Ill. "We're doing financial statements of forty companies—various divisions, subsidiaries, and partnerships. We're doing detailed operating statements for about 35 companies, using it as a cost system for about 15 companies; doing vouching for the 40 companies; and we're also doing consolidating."

The system Sorensen refers to, which Urban uses to implement its accounting and financial reporting system, was delivered four years ago by Applied Digital Technology, Inc., (ADTECH) a Chicago-based system house. The system consists of ADTECH software integrated with a General Automation SPC 16 minicomputer containing a 24K memory, a 25-megabyte disk drive, a 400-lpm printer, a card reader, and two keypunches.

According to Sorensen, there are two aspects to Urban's system. One is an accounts payable system; the other is a general ledger which, he says, is used for much more than that. "From the standpoint of software, it's one system, but we use it as if it's several different systems."

"Two things allow us to do that," he explained. "One is that . . . the generalized reporting part of the ADTECH system allows the user to define his own reports without needing a lot of programming experience. The other is the way we organized our chart of accounts to meet all the needs of cost reporting, financial reporting, financial statements, and operating statements. That means we have to control only one data base. And as long as we control that single data base, we know that all the reports are accurate."

He compared the system data base to a huge array of file drawers in which the user can file things in any way, with any number of indexes and tabs. And to extract that information at will.

Sorensen said that he joined Urban well after the system was installed so he wasn't involved with the system from the beginning. He recalls that there were a number of problems. "It took about six months for me to realize that most of the problems were in the way we were using the system. That's probably true with most systems," he added.

He said that data processing used to take about 30 percent of his time at Urban but now it takes an insignificant amount. "I have probably spent a total of 10 hours on data processing in the last year, but it took a lot of work to get the system to that point."

According to Sorensen, the basic structure of the file is such that it's completely data selective—the detail is never lost. "Every report that you've ever produced is reproducible from the basic data file. The basic data file consists of something they call transactions," he said. Once it's gone into the system it remains there. "There's nothing in the system to take it out unless I, as a user, choose to do so." It's this kind of control Sorensen likes. But with that control comes responsibility, according to Sorensen. "I would rather have those responsibilities and have the options as a user." He added that "It takes a certain philosophy to accept that as a user. It's much easier to sell a system to most people if you tell them the system is going to handle everything for you—you don't have to make any decisions. I think a lot of us get into traps when we accept that kind of system definition."

Urban is a leading real estate investment and development firm with offices in Chicago and Denver.

[*Infosystems*, December 1976, copyright © Hitchcock Publishing Co.]

## A TRANSPORT SERVICE

A small business system at Bruce's Transport Service in Ventura, Calif., has tripled the speed of cash flow for this company and will pay for itself in three years, according to William Aulich, accountant for the firm.

The company's primary business is hauling oil well drilling tools and equipment. As such, it is regulated by the Public Utilities Commission (PUC) as well as the Interstate Commerce Commission. The reports these agencies require are extensive; and in addition to keeping track of all general accounting details, the firm must keep tabs on miles driven, weight carried, and surcharges for each driver and each vehicle.

A small business system was clearly needed to provide this information. The company first installed an NCR Corp. 399 system which, according to Aulich, "never worked. We were very unhappy with the performance of both the hardware and software."

After eight months, the firm began surveying the field for another system that could do the job. It looked at IBM, Singer Business Machines, Burroughs Corp., and Digital Equipment Corp. systems and finally purchased a DEC Datasystem 310 in October 1976, Aulich reported.

The system was programmed by Mini Computer Business Applications of Los Angeles. The first set of programs was test run on the software vendor's mini, so "we were up and running as soon as we got the hardware in. The rest of the programs followed soon after."

The system will pay for itself in three years, Aulich predicted, through reduction in personnel needed, cut overhead, and faster turnaround time on invoices. Staff has already been cut in half.

"We're turning our records around daily now, instead of always being five, six, or seven days in arrears as we were when the accounts were being done by hand. Invoices which used to go out every three or four days are now going out daily.

"And since we're getting money back three times as fast, we're tripling the speed of cash flow," Aulich said. Payroll now takes three hours as compared with three days and accounts payable has been reduced to three hours from five days, he added.

Its versatility, dependability, and cost sold the company on the system and it's a decision the firm feels was well made. In fact, the PUC has asked other firms of this type to come look at the system at Bruce's, Aulich said.

[September 1977, copyright © *Computerworld*]

## AN ARCHITECTURAL PLANNING COMPANY

Minicomputer-aided design is helping Clifford Douglas Stewart Associates of Boston provide a range of services aimed at allowing architects to design what is needed where and when it is needed.

The architectural planning concern offers the use of its computer-aided design center to architects from other firms and also uses the system for its own work.

The company developed these services in order to help solve three problems in the construction industry: the great demand for construction, the shortage of experienced design specialists, and the reduced time span within which to provide these services.

The services provided cover a broad range. The system can help survey and map large areas to find appropriate building sites. The computerized data base contains information on the various characteristics of each area's natural resources. Selected criteria governing the potential use of land or selection of alternate sites can be displayed graphically.

The user selects the limits of interest within the appropriate criteria and a multitone map is plotted in up to three colors.

It can be used to analyze the socioeconomic forces in an urban environment. A variety of data is entered into memory and used selectively to generate shaded maps showing factors important to the planning effort. From basic plots, additional overlays can be requested of the computer until the final maps illustrate new considerations.

The system develops detailed listings of the space needs and planning requirements for educational, health, or industrial facilities. At the same time, lists of equipment, staffing profiles, and construction estimates can be compiled. For every space type in the building, a listing is maintained of the equipment and furnishings normally found in that space. This program delineates the description (including manufacturers); the required clearance dimensions, and the electrical, plumbing, gases, and exhaust requirements.

For each piece of equipment listed, there is a scaled drawing that can be called from memory, displayed on the CRT, and plotted in design or working drawing form on the plotter. Additional pieces can be added and simulations of movement and flow can be created dynamically and recorded.

The space program for a project can be assembled from the basic library in minutes, presenting the required area and the probable construction cost, escalated to bid date, for each major component of the program separated by phase of construction. Each edit of the proposed basic spaces illustrates the new relative cost, efficiency, and staffing requirements.

The most efficient layout of space can be discerned from computer-aided matrix analysis. The computerized approach eliminates the need for broad assumptions and guesswork in the site planning and interior layout of complex buildings. From a numerical code matrix representing the ideal relationship between each of the functions, the system generates a diagram of the ideal physical relationships. It then transforms the "bubbles" of the ideal diagram into exact scale rectangles of the correct dimension which the designer will arrange interactively on the CRT to form a proposed layout.

The systems behind these services are two Digital Equipment Corp. PDP-15s. The two minis stand side by side, but are completely independent. Each has 32K of core, disk cartridge drives, and an interactive graphics work station consisting of two CRTs, one with electronic tablet and spark pen, and a Versatec dot printer/plotter.

One system has a California Computer Products, Inc. (Calcomp) 36" three-pen plotter, for producing final ink drawings. Backup is done on magnetic tape, and data can be transferred between these and other similar systems on Dectape.

One of the two PDPs was purchased new from DEC. The other was purchased used. DEC maintains them both, including the Versatec and Calcomp plotters. Early in the development of the system, peripherals were purchased from and maintained by different manufacturers. This approach resulted in a lot of fingerpointing and time-wasting, trying to determine which piece of equipment had failed, and therefore which manufacturer was responsible for correcting the problem. Maintenance of the entire system by DEC resolved the problem of determination of responsibility.

The systems are used mainly by architects, not by programmers or other computer-oriented personnel. They are not in a very controlled environment; cigarettes and coffee are not forbidden. While this does occasionally cause a problem, it also results in greater acceptance of three- or four-hour-long work sessions at the work station.

[October 1977, copyright © Computerworld]

## A RADIO STATION

If there is a formula for good FM radio listening, the Susquehanna stations may have hit on it through a small computer.

Applying computer techniques to proven broadcasting parameters, Susquehanna Broadcasting Co. of York, Pa., is cutting weekly tapes for five FM stations that are turning listeners on in increasing numbers.

The parameters are simple enough. Songs and artists are separated so no particular one is played back to back or repeated in a four-hour time segment. Also, no half-hour tape is repeated in 68 hours—to avoid a selection being played in the same time slot.

Thus, a station does not follow one Frank Sinatra tune with another and the same Sinatra song will not be played again for at least four hours. And, the tape with the Sinatra piece slotted for 11 A.M. is not run again for 68 hours to avoid repeating the song in the same time frame.

"We could not do what we are doing on a manual basis," explains Robert B. Shipley, group FM program director. "This enables us to stay on target with the type of music we play and it controls repeats," he claims.

The Susquehanna approach is similar to that of the research laboratory where tests are conducted and the results are analyzed for flaws, re-examined, and tried until a logical solution is found. In the same vein, the computer goes through a trail and error process, matching and rejecting half-hour tapes until the log assembled meets Susquehanna requirements. One result has been an average of less than one hole per week to fill.

Susquehanna makes its program selections from thousands of musical standards, preparing half-hour tapes with selections balanced according to valid listening patterns and established popularity of titles. The company's five FM stations are furnished with several hundred numerically coded tapes, each containing breaks for news, weather, public service information, and commercial announcements. The company's tape-preparation system allows wide flexibility for each station to respond to major news developments or other local occurrences without difficulty. The number of each tape, its selections and artists, are captured on the computer's magnetic disk files.

Then, each Thursday, the computer, applying the program parameters, selects a week's tapes and prints a program log for each day's broadcasting beginning with the following Monday night. If there are any holes, they are filled in manually in York before the logs are distributed to the stations.

While the weekly log indicates when each tape is to be played, a computer list accompanying the tape details the selections, timing, and break points.

Besides serving the stations themselves, the computer draws on its disk files to print an alphabetic list of selections and the number of times they're on the tapes. Management uses the report to determine whether the songs are being featured in proportion to their popularity and in keeping with the company's ideas on good listening.

Another computer report shows the frequency with which each tape is being played. The information alerts the programming staff to examine why one tape may be getting more plays than another, or if a frequently broadcast tape may have outplayed its effectiveness.

When the computer is not assembling the program logs for the company's FM stations, it is doing the billing for Susquehanna's cable TV operations, CATV of York, and maintaining the accounts receivable records for seven AM and the five FM outlets.

Bills are prepared by the AM and FM stations and copies are sent to York, where the accounts receivable files are updated and aged and sales are analyzed. Aside from typing the bills, the local stations have nothing more to do with billing and accounts receivable paperwork.

On the other hand, the computer prepares the bills sent monthly to some 17,000 cable TV customers. Bills are prepared weekly on a cycle basis and receipts are posted at random daily, at which time the accounts are updated.

The bills are in continuous card format. The company has delayed making the bill a turnaround document because of a large number of exception payments and because the volume has not yet warranted it.

But the bill, according to Larry D. Potteiger, data processing manager, could easily be converted and Susquehanna can do the billing for several additional cable TV companies without appreciably increasing costs.

When orders are received, they are edited and the information is entered into the NCR Century 100. The computer stores the data and prints the necessary shipping copies/bills of lading and order register.

After the orders, which average 150 to 180 daily for all divisions, are shipped, the computer prints the invoices, updates the accounts receivable file, prepares an invoice register, and reduces inventories.

Sales and inventory reports are produced daily. Open orders, including current, future, and back orders, are reflected in the remaining available inventory. Applying set minimums, the production department can determine output needs.

The computer performs the usual aging that goes with every accounts receivable recordkeeping process. There are 20,000 customer records in the file. It also figures the commissions based on the sales information captured on entering the orders. Performance reports by customer and product sales forecasting are two other computerized summaries.

Bar graphs are prepared by the computer, which shows each line's production, orders, shipments, and inventory. The graphs are used by management in determining output cycles and work schedules.

The computer also processes the weekly payrolls for the manufacturing operation and the semimonthly pay records for the salaried radio personnel.

[March 1973, copyright © *Computerworld*]


## A MORTGAGE COMPANY

Mortgage loans are being "closed" much more quickly today than in the past at Wells Fargo Mortgage Co. in California. Recently, the company's closing department at its Santa Rosa service center changed from manual document preparation to an automated "closer" system installed by Radix Corp., Salt Lake City, Utah. Closing the average mortgage loan at Wells Fargo involves calculating interest, tax prorations, etc., and typing or printing some 40 documents including about 15 forms.

Much of Wells Fargo's daily operation was already under computer control prior to installing the Radix system, but mortgage closing was still at the typewriter/calculator stage. "We've had an IBM 370/125 for nearly four years," says Larry Bonin, data processing manager, "but it would have been inefficient to use a computer of this size to generate closing documents. Instead, we use the IBM for such applications as mortgage servicing, commitment control, and general ledger."

The system includes a 16K Datapoint 2200 work station; two Diablo cartridge disk drives capable of storing 2.5 million characters; two Datapoint cassette drives used for off-line storage of closed loans and for utility purposes; and a Perkin-Elmer Carousel 300 printer. The printer is a recent change in the Radix system, according to James E. Bagley, Radix vice-president, product development. Originally, the system used a printer from another vendor, but Radix switched to the Perkin-Elmer because of that company's "stronger commitment to maintenance and customer service," Bagley says.

"First we considered using a service bureau," Bonin relates, "but our volume was already too large to make it an economical proposition. We were also concerned about turnaround." Leasing a system was not feasible either, "because our costs of funds compare favorably with the rates of any leasing company, and we were confident that the system would satisfy our requirements for a number of years.

"Before we chose Radix, however, we took a good, hard look at several vendor's alternatives," Bonin comments. He says that some of them didn't offer after-sales service in the Santa Rosa area and none provided forms tailoring. "But Radix did. And this means we can alter our documents without programming intervention. The operator can now specify where the printing is to appear on the forms."

Once keyed, the operator visually verifies the input on the display. Each field can be automatically entered sequentially or manually in random order. After verification, pressing a function key transfers the data to disk, where it is stored until all documents for the loan are completed. Entered data can be altered any time before printing.

All information being complete and entered, the loan is ready for closing. First, the operator keys in the mortgage loan number to access the data. Then documents are selected and forms inserted into the Carousel. The Perkin-Elmer printing terminal interacts with the Datapoint 2200 to collect all the pertinent data for a particular document. Then the document is printed.

The 2200 and the Carousel can be operated both simultaneously and independently of each other because the printing terminal is programmable even though it operates under control of the 2200. To speed processing, the forms of similar-type mortgages can all be printed as a batch instead of producing all the forms of one loan before starting another, according to Bonin.

For example, a group of FHA loans can be processed together by the operator identifying, through the keyboard, all loans to be printed and then inserting all forms for printing such as all amortization tables, then all trust deeds, etc., for the entire group. After all documents for a loan have been produced, the relevant data is transferred from disk to cassette tape from which it can be retrieved and restored to disk if the loan documents must be redone for any reason.

[*Infosystems,* July 1977, copyright © Hitchcock Publishing Co.]


## A TRUCKING COMPANY

"I believe in multiple small systems because when the big one's down, everything is down," Dick Guyton, DP manager for Daily Express, Inc., of Carlisle, Pa., said in explaining how his firm has evolved into a user of two on-line minicomputers and one batch-oriented small business system.

The company is a specialized truck carrier that hauls

truckloads of farm gear, heavy machinery, and construction equipment.

The batch system, an NCR 101, is used to perform accounts receivable and payable, contractor settlements to pay contractors who deliver the loads, a self-insurance program, and fuel tax reporting, as well as to keep track of any areas with which regulated companies have to comply.

The two on-line Microdata Corp. Reality systems perform a motor truck dispatch application and also do the billing, accounts receivable and payable, and check-clearing activities for two other divisions of the company.

Daily Express has been computerized with the NCR equipment since 1970, but decided it needed to go on line to keep track of its motor dispatch application, Guyton said. Prior to the installation of the systems, dispatching had been done manually.

"We were handling the application with little pieces of paper stuck in slots in the wall," he recalled. "We had a plastic card that represented a trailer, and we had a 4-by-6 card that represented a power unit. Then, when we wrote up the work order, we would match the appropriate tractor with the appropriate trailer and put the loadcard with it.

"Then when you made an entry on the load card, you had to look for it, write the entry on it, and then pass it over to the entry department. So a lot of time was spent searching" for the card, he said.

Because communications costs were rising when it couldn't find the information needed to respond to phone calls and because it was having difficulty keeping track of its equipment, Daily Express turned to an on-line dispatch system.

An extensive search that took about two and a half years narrowed the field of available systems down to the Microdata Reality, Hewlett-Packard 2000, Interdata 8/32, and the Digital Equipment Corp. PDP-11. The Reality was chosen because of its operating system, Guyton said.

The first system was purchased from Keystone Data Systems, Inc., the Philadelphia-area Microdata dealer. A second system was bought later.

One of the on-line systems has 64K of memory and includes 25M bytes of disk storage, a magnetic tape system, and 24 communications ports. The other, also a 64K system, has only 20M bytes of disk, tape, 18 communications ports, and a printer.

The firm has about 28 CRTs in house. Outlying sites communicate with the system via 13 Decwriter teleprinters, several Teletype machines, and CRTs.

Programs were all written in house in BASIC, Guyton noted, because there were no packages available for "what we wanted to do." The Microdata English language is used for ad hoc report generation, he added.

Users of the dispatch application access an integrated data base which includes a load file, tractor file, and trailer file. When the sales department receives an order, it keys the information into the system through its CRTs.

The data entered includes load information and a complete description of the job. "We don't have a hard-copy load card, in effect," Guyton pointed out.

The information is then made available to the dispatchers. Scanning CRTs at their locations, they determine what resources are available, what loads they have to move, and when they have to move them and then assign equipment.

The act of assigning equipment simultaneously updates the tractor file, trailer file, and load file, Cuyton said.

When a trucker calls in after the truck has been loaded, the dispatchers input the actual weight and delivery data as well as any other information he might need to complete the delivery or the firm might need to produce a bill.

When the trucker empties the load, he calls a dispatcher, probably located in a remote location. The dispatcher keys in the driver's unit number and enters any final billing information needed.

The system also produces management reports such as trailer utilization reports and a pattern report which shows equipment types needed by "origin state" and "destination state" that attempts to point salespeople to where potential customers are likely to be located.

A position report gives the operations people and management an overview of what's happening and "is in effect a kind of a quickie backup."

"We are in the process of making it possible for the second system to absorb the workload of the first system" should the first system go down, Guyton said.

To do this requires a bit more disk storage. "We keep the 25M-byte disk on the dispatch Reality quite loaded, and the 20M-byte disk on the other Reality can't quite hold the system."

Anticipating a new operating system release for the system, Guyton said that as soon as it is distributed "we are going to dedicate the tape drive on the on-line system and, as we update a record, we will pass the updated records out with a peculiar key right to tape.

"That way, if we have a failure of the primary system, we would simply load the preceding day's saved files, update the files from the transaction log, and be back in business."

Management information is transferred daily to the NCR system through tapes, he noted.

Microdata takes care of the service of the system, he said, and "I have had absolutely no problem with it."

[August 1977, copyright © *Computerworld*]


## A KITCHEN ACCESSORIES SUPPLIER

This is a report about a business that experienced sharp growth in its five-year history. It needed more and better management information to develop growth strategies and to maximize its investment in sales and promotion. And further, it wanted to fine-tune its collection procedures, eliminate out-of-stock positions, and improve service to customers.

For Textol Co., Inc., Irving, Tex., the answers came in the form of a small in-house business computer. According to Leonard Yanigan, Textol president, the company had tried service bureaus and time-sharing services and found they couldn't handle overloads and still provide management information reports. As a company that internationally sells all-fabric placemats, napkins, and cloth kitchen accessories, under such brand names as Quiltees and Giftkins, it needed more.

The system selected, according to Yanigan, is "a one-operator integrated system efficiently handling our work orders, invoicing, cash receipts, inventory, account aging, salesmen's commissions, and management reporting. The two bookkeeper/typists who previously processed the work orders and invoices have been released to other tasks, and one employee, who previously worked part time in the plant as a folder and part time as a clerk in the office, is our computer operator."

He went on to say, "We have managed the maneuver from manual to computerized systems without the need to hire programming or other computer-experienced personnel and, importantly, without the need to adapt our proven procedures to the needs of a service bureau. We are simply doing the critical work order, invoicing, cash receipts, and inventory tasks much faster, with fewer people, and are getting as a vital by-product the information needed to manage growth."

Hardware consists of Century Computer's Opus III base unit with 32K of internal memory, a Model 030 eight-port multiplexer, a medium-speed line printer, a 10-megabyte disk memory unit, and one CRT terminal with standard keyboard. Software for the system comprises the Century Application Program for general ledger accounting, order writing and invoicing, inventory accounting, accounts payable, and sales analysis.

Customer, product, and salesman's master files were created during the initial phase of the installation at the Textol office. The customer master file has information about each customer, such as country, state, city, tax information, terms code, price code, salesman's number, credit data, date of last purchase, date of last payment, gross sales, bill-to address, ship-to address, and aged balance, if any.

The product master file tabulates individual product information in product number sequence and contains information on price, beginning inventory, date of last receipt and last sale, current stock balance, and sales and amount details, as well as month-to-date and year-to-date sales and costs.

According to Yanigan, "The operator enters the order information in English language. When an order is completed, she simply instructs the system to print the required documents, including invoicing and shipping documents. Ordered items are automatically deducted from inventory. Back orders are handled in similar fashion. The invoice register is printed on a daily basis, and has a one-line summary of each invoice generated. The cash receipts register, also printed daily, identifies each cash receipt by reference number, date, and amount. Each day the totals applied to each salesman's commission balance is also reported, and the system prints out the information on commissions, which is sent to the individual salesman."

In addition, the Opus III system provides an aged accounts receivable report which lists, by customer, all monthly transactions, giving the date, reference number, and amount for each transaction. The aged accounts receivable summary condenses receivables information into charges, credits, current and aged totals, and balance due.

"The small business computer system we have installed is both an operating and a management tool. It is enabling Textol to meet the problems of growth within a cost and personnel framework that is feasible for a company of this size—and it is yielding, at low cost, the kind of information that management needs to plot its future growth course," concludes Yanigan.

[*Infosystems,* April 1977, copyright © Hitchcock Publishing Co.]

## A BUILDING MATERIALS OUTLET

Last year, Bob Poe decided it was time to find a better way to quickly determine the profitability of his business. Manual accounting procedures no longer gave him the timely management information and reports he needed for control. Poe owns Poe Lumber Company, a firm of retail outlets selling building materials and supplies in southern Indiana. Annual sales volume runs about $4 million.

A small business computer provided part of the solution. In this case the total solution was the combination of the right hardware and the right software: turnkey hardware that lent itself to easy operation and a special application program package tailored for retail businesses like Poe's.

Poe Lumber employs 60 in three retail outlets. The main store (and home office) is in Marengo, about 30 miles west of Louisville, Ky. There are stores in Ramsay (15 miles from Marengo) and in Paoli (20 miles away). The concrete plant at the Marengo yard is treated as a fourth location for accounting purposes.

In his search for the system that would best meet his needs, Poe thoroughly investigated models of several vendors. Several requirements were especially important to him. The system had to be easy for present employees to learn and operate. The system had to be easily understood by all employees who handled paperwork, so they could easily adjust to the change from manual paperwork to data processing, particularly in the handling of sales slips, inventory records, and invoices. The system had to process batched transactions from all four locations at the home office and still provide next-day and periodic reports needed to determine current profitability.

The system Poe selected, and purchased outright, was a Link 100 from Randal Data Systems, Inc. His final choice rested on three main factors: the hardware, the software, and the price. Components of the Link 100 system include a processor, a visual display terminal, a printer, and storage for up to four floppy disks (which hold all files needed to process daily transactions: program, customer file, inventory, and daily work: accounts payable and payroll are on separate files).

Each day a Poe driver picks up the daily sales slips, inventory receipts, and other necessary paperwork from each of the locations and brings them back to the home office in the afternoon. From them, the terminal operator enters the data into the system.

Software, especially important in Poe's selection of a small computer system, came in the form of a specially designed package. The Buildings Material Industry Management Control System had been developed by George McMurtry, then a distributor of small business computers in Indianapolis (he has since joined the Randal organization).

The BMI-MCS package was designed to provide the special management information and control for executives in the building supply industry. It handles both retail and wholesale operations. Besides lumber and building materials, the package is also suited for other businesses, such as electrical supplies, industrial supplies, plumbing, heating, and air conditioning, and office products dealers.

The big benefit of automation for Poe was that it enabled him to more quickly determine gross profitability and comparisons to budget, almost on a daily basis, and net profits right at the end of each month, something manual methods couldn't provide. Ernie Stroud, who supervises the system, also pointed out that automation helped establish operating and procedural disciplines that have saved clerical time and provided accuracy checks. Any time during the month, the system can provide the status of any customer account, because receivables are updated daily; statement preparation and aged account balances are produced almost automatically.

[*Modern Office Procedures,* October 1977, copyright © Penton/IPC, subsidiary of Pittway Corporation]

## AN AUTO PARTS SUPPLIER

A small business system has enabled National Set Screw Corp. (NSS) of Plymouth, Mich., to increase its sales almost 400 percent in four years without adding administrative help, according to Peter Ewing, president.

Programmed by the president himself, the system performs accounting, inventory, management, order entry, and job cost estimation functions. Employees in various locations can simultaneously access programs and data stored in a central system through remote work stations.

In a key application the system also figures how much money it costs per day to use a particular machine for a particular job to allow the company to find out what jobs are profitable.

In 1973 the firm, which supplies parts for the auto and construction industries, reported sales of $1.5 million. Sales rose from that figure to an excess of $6 million in the most recent fiscal year.

"We achieved this increase in our sales without adding any more administrative staff," Ewing noted. "The Datapoint 2200 system we installed in 1974, plus the additions we have made to the unit in the meantime, have enabled us to raise the productivity of existing personnel to handle the increased workload," he said.

"Our out-of-pocket savings have been tremendous," he added. "Additional people would have cost us substantially more than the Datapoint investment but would not have produced the same results. As we see it, the equipment is not just a money saver, it's a money maker."

NSS began its internal computing operation with a single Datapoint 2200 system in September 1974. Before settling on the Datapoint 2200 processor, Ewing made a comprehensive study of all the small business computers available at that time.

Ewing looked at small business systems and bare-bones minis alike, including systems from Digital Equipment Corp., Burroughs Corp., Basic Four Corp., Varian Data Systems, and IBM. Systems from both Microdata and Datapoint came closest to fulfilling the need; the Datapoint was chosen on price and software considerations. As Ewing pointed out, "IBM has nothing comparable to it for under $300,000."

He said no other maker offered the comprehensive operating system and sophisticated programming languages available on the 2200. "I was especially impressed by the DATABUS language, with which I have written almost all of the programs involved here."

Another key benefit of the system, from Ewing's point of view, is economy of operation. "I absolutely did not want to add a DP manager to our staff. With the aid of the 2200, a couple of sharp secretaries and I have been able to handle the entire operation," he said.

The original 2200 installation has now been upgraded to allow several users to access the processor at one time. The Datashare system incorporates not only the 2200 but two cartridge disk drives for data and program storage, a printer, and five Datapoint 3600 CRT work stations. The work stations are located in various offices at NSS.

Ewing plans to increase the capability of the system again by putting in a large Datapoint 5500 processor to allow more terminals to be attached and to gain quicker response time, he said. The firm also purchased a Tektronic, Inc. 4501 graphics terminal to help its engineers, emphasizing its commitment to user-oriented DP.

The basis for NSS' in-house activity is the purchase order, which usually arrives in the mail. The company currently receives approximately 1,000 purchases a month, all of which are entered into the system through a single unit in the company's administrative offices.

"My secretary can handle the purchase orders in a few hours each morning," Ewing stated. "Under our previous system, this amounted to a full-time job for at least one clerk and other less qualified help."

Ewing's secretary uses a 3600 work station to enter purchase order information into a computerized filing system. The video screen displays a menu, or an entry format for the data, which helps secure error-free data input. Should errors be made during the data input process, the unit is programmed to signal the operator and initiate reentry of the data.

Finished goods inventories are checked by the mini and a

stock-pull issued. If the item is not in stock, the order is entered into the NSS production schedule and a request for raw material is inserted.

NSS executives receive a daily printout of jobs in progress and their current status. Managers need a daily printout of this file so that they can determine the status of any particular job and, at the same time, get an accurate overview of company progress in sales and deliveries.

The order entry log, also prepared at periodic intervals, provides company executives with current information on orders in process. This enables them to handle production scheduling more efficiently and to maintain and replenish necessary stocks of raw materials and other parts.

The file of order entries also provides information for sales and analyses, including the movement of particular products, the performance of sales representatives, and territorial and industry performance. When goods are shipped, the same file is used as the basis for preparation of the appropriate invoices.

The order entry information provides a basis for the production scheduling process, which is under the direction of Paul Ewing, Peter's brother and partner in this family-owned business. "To increase our productivity, we must accurately assess—on the basis of manpower requirements, machine availability, and, especially, stocks of raw materials and other commodities—what the manufacturing situation will be two, three, or four months from now," he explained.

"If you guess wrong here, other variables such as raw stock prices, which can fluctuate rapidly, will eat you right up."

NSS has completely converted its stock inventory to the Datapoint system and is currently converting its work-in-progress to the computerized approach. "The company," Ewing pointed out, "will reap major benefits from having all its materials inventory maintained and updated by the system. We will be better able to adjust our production scheduling and sales forecasting to the buying process. We will then have the stock when we need it and won't be so vulnerable to price fluctuations and materials shortages. This will also help us to make sure that we do not have capital tied up in dormant inventory."

Peter Ewing learned the DATABUS language in a few hours' time through study of the manual provided by Datapoint. "I did take some computer programming courses," he acknowledged, "but that was some time ago."

Ewing noted that while the Datashare system has helped the company in many ways, it has been especially helpful in the area of job follow-ups. "We used to keep a card file on each job we had going, and as the number of jobs we handled increased, it got to be a three-ring circus trying to keep tabs on everything," he said.

"When customers called and asked about the status of their orders or why an order hadn't been delivered on time, I used to spend half my day tracking down the jobs and finding out what the trouble was. Quite often my efforts were hampered by misfiled or lost job cards; that can't happen now. With the minicomputer, all that information is stored on a consolidated file which can be accessed immediately. It has enabled me to make much more productive use of my time."

[August 1977, copyright © *Computerworld*]

## A SEAFOOD IMPORTER

Like finding the proverbial pearl in an oyster, Ocean Garden Products, Inc. of San Diego, Cal. has netted an unexpected bonus by using its small business system for an unplanned application.

The frozen seafood importer originally bought its system to handle routine accounting functions. The system has since been given the extra job of controlling sales traffic by determining which cases in a given warehouse should be removed to fill incoming orders and then issuing sales invoices as the goods are shipped.

Founded 20 years ago, the firm has been using computers for accounting for more than a decade, according to controller Frank Barrancotto. At one time an IBM System 360 was leased but "it was too big and too expensive. However, our sorting and computational needs are so high that nothing smaller would do," he said.

A switch to a service bureau followed, with Ocean Garden personnel punching cards that were sent to the bureau for handling. "This had drawbacks, too," Barrancotto said, "since it didn't give us an interactive capability, which is particularly important in terms of checking customer records or reviewing transactions. The service bureau was performing a simple historical function compiling data."

In mid-1972, Ocean Garden had a management consultant conduct a study to determine an economical, flexible accounting system. Initially, a Basic/Four Model 400 was recommended, and since then the company has upgraded to a Model 600.

The Model 600 is at the food company's headquarters to prepare data for the IBM 360 used at the local service bureau. This enables the accounting department to work with elementary data in its offices, yet have the 360 to process as much as 100,000 records at a time.

The present Model 600 system consists of one CPU, six CRTs, two 200 line/min. printers, one paper tape punch, one magnetic tape, and two disk drives.

About a year after installation of the original system, Barrancotto and his staff began toying with the notion of using the computer to handle sales traffic from the warehouses in which Ocean Garden stores its imported frozen products. The sales inventory control system went live in September 1976.

In discussing the order entry aspects of the system, Barrancotto explained that as orders are received, sales information is typed onto the video display terminal and entered into the customer files. While this data is being reviewed and adjusted, the system is also performing accounts receivable functions. The Basic/Four system maintains a perpetual physical inventory of what lots of products are in which warehouses, and a salesman decides from which warehouse to take the goods, but the computer selects the cases to take.

The decision is based on three criteria:

- The lot storage dates and when the space rental for various cases will lapse.
- The age of the products, based on when they entered the United States.
- The size of the lot being ordered in relation to the tariff structure of the specific warehouse.

In what Barrancotto describes as an unusual process, the minicomputer punches out tape to drive a remote printer that advises the warehouse on which lots to pull and where to send them. This same information is also used by the mini to produce written confirmation records for the broker or the firm's own sales office, the trucker who will transport the shipment, the warehouse from which it's released, and the final destination.

"Our sales inventory system plus the computer's ability to weight 40 to 50 lots in seconds contributes to the most efficient use of our inventories," Barrancotto concluded.

[September 1977, copyright © *Computerworld*]

## A BROKERAGE FIRM

Working with thousands of different numbers, hundreds of different clients, 76 CRTs, and two minicomputers, J.J. Kenny Co., Inc. of New York, a municipal bond brokerage firm, provides the critical link between buyer and seller in the secondary bonds market.

Referring to itself as "the broker's broker," the company provides municipal bond information within five minutes to dealers and dealer banks with its automated system.

J.J. Kenny has two Digital Scientific Corp. Meta 4 minicomputers, which emulate the IBM 1130. They are linked to Computer Communications, Inc. (CCI) CRTs at each trader's desk.

The company is so enthusiastic about its computerized operations, there are 76 CRTs for its 86 employees scattered around the headquarters building, according to Richard Donnelly, vice-president and secretary.

As a municipal bond bid comes in over the telephone to a trader, he types in all the necessary information on the CRT. The CRT then displays all the daily bids available according to their declining dollar amount.

The client decides when the best price is reached and sells to the highest bidder if he wishes to. The system records, stores, and invoices all the information.

The transaction is completed and the system work is ended when the bonds are delivered and paid for, Donnelly explained.

J.J. Kenny never sees the actual bond but only works as the intermediary between the buyer and seller in conjunction with a clearing agent, according to Donnelly.

The system was designed to handle the constant flow of information. After the bid-wanted item is taken via the telephone, the trader rechecks a description of the item for accuracy and it is input to the CRT, which transmits it over the firm's private teleprinter system reaching 87 cities.

Once the item goes over the system, traders at J.J. Kenny wait for the calls to start coming in. Within several hours of the start of business one day, J.J. Kenny already had received 673 bids worth $25 million on file and transacted 17 bids worth $3.2 million; the system had been accessed by traders 6,441 times.

On an average day, the company handles $40 million to $60 million worth of bonds.

The public is not told who sells the bonds or who buys them, since the company maintains a strict sealed-bid policy, officials said.

The system has the ability to work in three modes— yesterday, today, and tomorrow—according to Donnelly. The complete bidding and sales of the previous day can be called up and tomorrow's program can be readied while work on the present day's bid is being done, he said.

The system relieves the trader of detail so he can handle other business, cover accounts better, handle more calls, obtain a wider range of information, and avoid number-crunching problems, Donnelly said.

Using this method, the trader has more time to handle the negotiations between buyer and seller, he added.

J.J. Kenny's primary work consists of handling the bid-wanted items and the active trading market.

The company keeps three minicomputer systems in house, two in its DP center, and one in its subsidiary Municipal Security Evaluation Service (MSES). Both companies have real-time, data-base-oriented systems.

Previously, J.J. Kenny used an IBM 1130 system but because of the company growth needed faster throughput. In 1971, it converted from batch processing to CRTs and then went to real time, ordering its first Meta 4 to emulate the 1130, Donnelly said.

The company did several benchmark tests before buying the Meta 4s but was most pleased with that system's performance, he added. Many other systems were still in the development stage at that time, he recalled.

The company also upgraded to on-line communications, added disks, firmware, and software. It can keep adding terminals without a decrease in throughput, he said.

The bid information that is input into the CRT includes the time the trade took place, where the bid was taken, which trader took it, the bond description, the owner, the percentage yield and concession.

Other information includes when the date of the bond will mature, the region it's from, state, and interest rate.

The daily list of municipal bond offerings is stored on disk for fast availability. The system also stores information on blocks of bonds for the bond yield and its dollar equivalent.

The system can also scan all available resources to find the bond that fits a specific inquiry, Donnelly said.

After trading has stopped for the day, the system continues to work to confirm and verify all the bond trades that occurred that day. The verification process includes data on which security bond was bought and sold, the price, and the accrued interest.

The system also provides an internal communications network to send messages to an individual or to every trader on the floor. This network is important, since noise level directly affects the work done by the trader, who must listen and record many bits of information via the telephone. The message can also be recalled if a trader missed it when it first was called up.

The two systems and front ends, which include a CCI channel adapter and multiplexer, are valued at $600,000, according to Donnelly. Besides the Meta 4 minis and front ends, the system includes a card reader, disk drives, paper tape unit, and magnetic tape.

The two Meta 4s share a Kennedy magnetic tape controller; the disk drives can be switched between the two computers. Both computers are fully redundant and are used as backup to each other, Donnelly said, adding the batch card reader system has been kept as a further backup system.

The system stores 130 data files for use by a trader at any time.

The data is copied continually; every half-hour all the data is printed so it can be stored off site. The trading information is taken off site daily and software is also kept off site.

[December 1977, copyright © *Computerworld*]


## A MINICONGLOMERATE

Many firms are standardizing and streamlining their DP and management activities using small systems. A case in point is Cetec Corp., a miniconglomerate headquartered in El Monte, Cal., that manufactures electronics, including broadcast equipment, component supplies, marine and computer products, and plastic extrusions.

Realizing rapid growth without the proper management controls can bring with it a number of problems such as a lack of communications among the divisions, repetition of certain tasks, and overall inefficiency, the company was reorganized into 12 independent profit centers with a mutual data base so each division manager has all the knowledge he needs to handle his operation.

At the same time, this organization provides a common source of information for the entire company with data only entered once.

In order to accomplish this, the firm has installed four Basic/Four Corp. small business computers; future plans call for the addition of four more systems. While there were a number of reasons for choosing this particular manufacturer, one of the primary advantages to the small systems is their interactive capability.

If a user has to rely on a service bureau or batch processing for data processing, chances are the information is out of date by the time he has access to it. With an interactive system, the output is as current as the last transaction. All management decisions are made on the latest statistics.

Another major reason for selecting these particular systems was to minimize software expenses by standardizing the programs and the programming language throughout the divisions.

Before the present systems were installed, Cetec's information systems varied from automated to manual. For example, the Sparta Division used a Honeywell 57, while the Benmar Division used an IBM System 3.

Typical of the situation was Moltronics, a distributor of electric components to industrial accounts with four locations in California and Arizona. This division used a manual inventory control and purchasing system with a combination of hand-posted records, cardex, and bin cards.

Nine-part packing slip/invoice forms were typed on a Friden Flexowriter, then extended, journalized, and posted to accounts receivable on an NCR 395 accounting system.

Moreover, there was no common system either operationally or for accounting purposes at the four locations, so the end result was four independent businesses.

The initial small business system at Moltronics was a

Basic/Four Model 350 with one CRT, one high-capacity disk drive, and a medium-speed printer for hard-copy reports, packing slips, invoices, and checks. Since that time Moltronics' sales volume has doubled and the system upgraded to a Model 500 with three high-capacity disk drives, three medium-speed printers, five CRTs, and a communications interface. User memory is 48K bytes with 12.6M bytes on-line storage.

The current configuration has a CRT located in the Moltronics San Diego facility and one CRT and printer at both the Phoenix and Santa Clara locations, while the CPU, disk drives, printer, and two CRTs are at the main plant in South Gate, Cal.

A line is reserved 24 hours a day for on-line real-time inventory stock checks, and order entry.

In addition to performing order entry and controlling inventory, the business functions currently handled by the systems include bill-of-material processing, material requirements planning, job costing, sales analysis, accounts payable and receivable, and payroll.

[*Computerworld*, January 1978, copyright © CW Communications/Inc.]

## A BROADCASTING COMPANY

In Bismarck, N.D., all of Meyer Broadcasting Co.'s advertisement scheduling and business functions are being run on its in-house business system, which has helped the company gain control of a complex and fast-moving business, according to its president, William Ekberg.

In terms of numbers, Meyer Broadcasting's listening audience is not large; geographically, however, it covers five states and two Canadian provinces, giving it the widest-ranging daytime coverage in the United States.

And with three television stations, three FM radio stations, three AM stations, and two cable TV systems, automation is essential to the company, Ekberg believes. "I don't know how we could get along without a computer anymore," he said.

Meyer Broadcasting uses an IBM System 3 Model 12 for its cable TV billing, product and sales analysis, accounts receivable, general ledger, payroll, and accounts payable. But its most critical job is scheduling the radio and TV commercials.

An advertiser may want a specific time slot or a varying one, so the system must be flexible as well as accurate, Ekberg said. The 3/12 has been programmed so it can rotate a commercial vertically—so it runs at different times—and horizontally—so it runs on different days each week.

Horizontal scheduling "is a better buy than if the message ran at 7 P.M. every Wednesday for seven weeks—the people who watch the Wednesday night movie would see it every week for seven weeks and the people who don't watch the movie would never see the message," Ekberg said.

The system can rotate the ads automatically—a task nearly impossible to do manually with 600 to 700 weekly spots, according to Ekberg.

The system also indicates what spots have already been sold, what is available, and what the advertiser's priorities are. Further, it produces Meyer Broadcasting's program log weeks in advance. If an interruption for a special broadcast occurs and a message has to be rescheduled, the system reschedules the entire log.

The small system also prints a confirmation sheet showing which commercials have been aired. In addition, it prints out advertiser contracts that detail the value and number of all daily spots.

The three TV stations are operated in a mother station/satellite mode, according to Ekberg. KFYR in Bismarck is the mother station; all national advertising as well as network programing and the first half of the noon, 6 P.M., and 10 P.M. news and weather are broadcast and fed straight through to the other stations.

The system is therefore responsible for that share of ad scheduling to all the stations, although the second half of the news programs and their commercials are handled separately by each station.

Two AM radio stations in Montana use IBM System 32s in stand-alone operations that aren't connected to the System 3 in Bismarck.

Meyer Broadcasting first began using data processing in 1966 with an IBM 402. As its needs became more complex, it upgraded from the 402 to a System 3 Model 6, then to a Model 10, and finally to its present Model 12, installed about a year and a half ago.

At the time Meyer Broadcasting automated, there were few specialized data services, so it decided to build its own system. Now it is happy with its added flexibility in producing reports and generating new data, according to Ekberg.

"When you work with a data servicer, you are more or less locked into the services it can provide you. We wanted to do some things our way," he said.

One extra feature is the system-generated sales report, which gives national and regional spot sales access to a whole block of time. Allowing two days for adjustments, the last five days are frozen and the time is given over to local advertisers. This has resolved conflicts at the sales level, according to Ekberg, and was easy to do because of the controlled in-house environment.

One reason the company chose IBM as its vendor was its availability. There aren't a lot of different computer companies in this area, Ed Kautzman, head of DP operations, noted. But the service has been very good even with the long distances, he added.

Meyer's 3/12 system includes dual programming, 80K memory, dual disk drives, five CRTs, and telecommunications between the TV stations.

"Our next step is to go on line in all our applications," Ekberg said. All keypunching will soon be eliminated and all the input will be via CRTs, he added.

Real-time information will give Meyer Broadcasting the ability to immediately know where it stands at all times in its commercial scheduling, Ekberg said.

[*Computerworld,* January 1978, copyright © CW Communications/Inc.]

## A TRAVEL FIRM

Besides solving problems for which a turnkey system is purchased, a user often reaps unexpected dividends. The case of Rogal Associates is a good example. It bought a system that reduced the paperwork load and, as a fringe benefit, reduced their clients' paperwork.

Rogal Associates, a wholesale travel firm based in Newton Center, Mass., specializes in group and incentive travel programs for large companies like General Electric, Hotpoint, and ITT. The firm has 16 employees handling an average of three charter plane loads a week, annual sales in the $10 million range, and plenty of paperwork. The business of putting together a group tour involves continuous document preparation. From the minute an application arrives to the time final payments are received, the passenger's name, address, and passport number must be alphabetized and typed continuously. This data is used for a variety of lists, mailings, airline manifests, hotel registrations, boarding passes, and option coupons.

Vice-president Bruce Rogal was concerned about the growing workload. In addition to the inherent paperwork in his business, he still had his own payables, receivables, and payroll. During the heavy season, he was employing five extra part-time staffers; looking ahead to business growth, he could foresee hiring an additional five full-time clerks, plus renting additional office space to accommodate a larger staff. It seemed like a logical time to automate, and Rogal began studying available systems.

He settled on a Basic/Four Model 350 central processor, disk drive, CRT terminal, and high-speed printer. All hardware is modular, so he can add memory capacity or peripherals at any time. The initial systems were developed by Rogal Associates working closely with the local Basic/Four branch office. Rogal wanted the manufacturer to provide finished systems, but also wanted his staff to become familiar with the BASIC programming language so that some of the future changes could be done right in-house. Operations are simple; existing staff members can usually learn to operate a particular application in 15 to 20 minutes.

The prime application takes care of all paperwork necessary for booking a tour. Working right from the client's application, an operator keys in the client's name, address, membership date and status, deposit receipt, and the options that the client wants for his trip. The computer takes it from there. It produces an invoice for the client, and sets up an account receivable. Just prior to the trip, it produces an alphabetized hotel room list, assigning rooms and adjacencies. Next it prints out an alphabetized airline boarding manifest, plus individual boarding passes for all group members. It prints out option coupons, plus a master list showing who gets what options. Finally, it prints a set of mailing labels to mail each tour group member his documents.

While all these functions are going on, the travel agency can still use the machine for all of its accounting:

- Accounts receivable
- Accounts payable
- Cash disbursements
- Payroll and taxes

With the finished system doing all that Rogal expected, he found that it had extra capacity that could be used to advantage. The simple programming allowed him to set up special systems in a short time. For example:

- He can perform special tasks for client companies. Even though these may be large companies with large-scale computers, Rogal's smaller system has greater flexibility for specialized programs.
- He can operate a quota award system for a client company, thus sparing the client company the task of keeping track of the salespeople who qualify for incentive travel plans.
- Using the computer, the travel firm can handle special large operations that are beyond the scope of manual

operations. As an example, Rogal recently handled all operations for the 8th International Congress of Child Psychiatrists, a group of 2,000 from all over the world. A convention of this size requires storage and processing of tremendous quantities of operating and accounting data.

- Rogal has found the computer to be a strong selling point for prospective customers. Most other travel companies require the client company that is paying for the tour to do much of the internal paperwork for the employees who are taking the trip: passport numbers, names, and the like. In short, the client is forced to act as his own travel agent. Rogal Associates can eliminate all of this paperwork for clients, so the incentive buyer has only to decide on the trip. The computer does the rest.

[*Modern Office Procedures,* July 1975, copyright © Penton/IPC, subsidiary of Pittway Corporation]

## A HOTEL OPERATOR

Resort Inns of America, the owner and operator of several hotels in St. Petersburg Beach, Fla., is using a small business system to gain increased control over its diverse business.

The company owns not only the hotels but also retail shops, an advertising agency, a hotel-oriented supply corporation, and other hotel-related companies.

"Resort Inns of America is a rapidly growing corporation," Don Elliott, treasurer and controller explained. Because of that rapid growth, it decided it needed to automate, so it purchased a Century Computer, Inc. small business system.

"We became acquainted with Century when we bought one of its small tape computers from a dealer. The dealer has since become defunct and we have become a quasi-dealer ourselves," Elliott explained.

Presently the company has a larger, disk-based model. The disk-based system is responsible for the bookkeeping processing of three subsidiary corporations. It records and analyzes guest reservations for all five motels, records and analyzes all prior guest reservations for the past two years, follows through on promotional mailings to these prior guests, records and analyzes travel agent business (and follows through on personalized mailings to some 10,000 agents), and performs statistical analysis of all inquiries and the business that results from the inquiries.

"All programming is done by operating staff and input is accomplished by regular office personnel. We have telecommunications to the computer from the motels and two CRT terminals in the office," Elliott said.

Two members of management have portable terminals which enable them to communicate with the system from their homes, so "it is not unusual for input and querying to be going on over a 12-hour period," he said.

Basic accommodations data for the motels is housed in master files. Other files hold guest names (the chain does a 50 percent repeat business) and house the names and accounts of travel agents.

Reservations are centrally recorded and entered into the system daily, with a simultaneous entry made in the appropriate travel agent's file, updating his account.

"The Century 400 system prints out the reservations for the arrivals scheduled at each motel for the following day," Elliott said. "The system also prints out at scheduled intervals the labels for direct mail to previous guests."

Basic software for the system was provided by Century. Hardware consists of the CPU, 32K bytes of internal memory, 16-port multiplexer, two medium-speed line printers, one 10M-byte disk drive and disk controller, two CRT terminals with standard keyboards, and the portable terminals.

[October 1977, copyright © *Computerworld*]


# A REAL ESTATE AGENCY

A minicomputer has proved to be the key to opening doors for real estate agents in Melville, N.Y.

The system, located at Multiple Listing Service of Long Island, Inc. (MLS), has been credited with making the job of finding the right house for the right client more efficient.

MLS is an amalgamation of 659 participating offices in the resale home market in Queens, Nassau, and Suffolk counties.

Of all the minicomputer's functions, the one that seems to trigger the most sales is a residential analysis done on the portable terminals the agents use. One broker reported the analysis has brought him a minimum of one home sale a month—at an average price of $60,000—since the system was installed in April.

The analysis is often the clincher for the prospect who isn't sure he can afford the home, according to Val Mason of Butterfield Realty. The prospect is asked to provide the amount of his monthly rent and his estimated income. Once this data has been entered, the terminal prints out the price he can afford without spending more than he does now.

The terminal also prints the income tax benefits which will accrue based on his real estate tax rate and what his equity will be over the next five or ten years based on amortization and a 5 percent increment for use "appreciation."

For example, a father of one earning $20,000 a year and paying $375 a month for rent finds that the same payment will bring him (after a downpayment of $9,000) a $45,000 house in which, based on the formula, he will have a $23,055.90 equity in five years and a $41,402 equity in ten years.

According to realtors, the terminal's printout of these compilations is generally seized upon by the prospect for further study at home.

The bread-and-butter function of the system, and one which relates directly to MLS's prime function, is the listing update.

With the system, all listings received from the association are entered into the mini and are immediately available to the terminal subscribers. Members not on the system receive their information by messenger up to 24 hours later.

Because of the competitive edge it gives them, many of the subscribers request the listing updates three times a day.

Subscribing agents can also enter their prospects' requirements—such as number of rooms, baths, and preferred neighborhood—by code so that another agent can search through them. If he has anything which satisfies the requirements, he can then contact the prospect's agent and suggest that a particular home listing with the calling agent be shown.

On the selling side, through its ability to list "comparables"—what similar houses have sold for and are currently seling for—the system helps agents keep their clients attuned to reality.

When a homeowner comes in to list a house, he often has an inflated idea of what it will bring. The system can print out a list of comparable homes which are on the market now and against which his home is, in effect, competing.

Since it was introduced in April, the system has grown consistently. So far, approximately 18 percent of MLS's membership has signed up. According to Margot Wolf, "that is about the number of agents and clerical employees which can be trained at MLS headquarters in Melville, Long Island."

The only charge for the system is $158 per month for the terminal.

The only complaint about the system is that when the new listings come in—seconds after they have been entered—they lack the photograph that is a standard part of the manually distributed hard copy.

However, as one broker pointed out, "We are beginning to find out that the lack of the photo is an advantage. If we get a match between a listing and what the prospect has asked for we can tell him we've got just what he asked for.

"Sometimes with the photograph we tell the prospect that and he says 'Yes. That's what I asked for, but I don't like it.' "

The system is a Hewlett-Packard 21MX, programmed by Realtronics, Inc. of McLean, Va.

[July 1977, copyright © *Computerworld*]

## A FOOD SUPPLIER

Because "we didn't want to get locked into a type of thinking in which we were going to serve the computer instead of the computer serving us," Bob Jones Corp. of Grand Rapids, Mich., had its small business system programmed by a company that had an "open mind," according to Bob Tourek, president of the company.

The firm went the small business system route after using a service bureau for several years and even doing some in-house keypunching. It chose an IBM System 32 after looking at several alternatives. It "was the only one that could fulfill a secretarial function," Tourek stated.

Then the firm searched for a programming company to fill its needs. Several were suggested by IBM, and after interviewing representatives from all of them, Bob Jones chose Computer Directions, Inc. The firm was just starting out, Tourek explained, and it was flexible enough to see the computer as a tool for solving sales problems.

The system, which captures and maintains data on sales histories to produce a number of reports, prints the reports in a format that is easily understood by both the salespeople and the customers.

Other reports compare year-to-date sales figures for the current year and the previous year as well as the sales figures for the same three months of the previous year. This allows the company to evaluate sales for the current year in relationship to the same period last year and plan sales tactics, he explained.

Promotion reports are used to help account for large fluctuations in sales and to evaluate the success of specific types of promotions.

The system also provides trend reports comparing average weekly movement for the previous 52 weeks with similar figures for the prior 52 weeks. These reports, detailing the movement by item for specified customers, identify trends, distribution holes, and new distributions.

The system is also being used to maintain data on brokerages due. Sales volumes and brokerage receipts can be reported by customer type (grocery, nonfoods, and food service) or by item type (grocery, frozen, dairy, meat, and nonfoods).

Reports are produced on demand, thus eliminating the unnecessary production of paper volume. The parameters for the reports are entered by the operator so that reports can be limited to certain time periods, certain principals, or certain items, Tourek said.

The data for the system is obtained from orders and invoices. Customer orders are entered on the computer, and orders are printed for mailing to the principals.

Daily and weekly reports are printed to provide order volume data and to compare this week's orders to those for the corresponding week from last year.

When invoices are received, only the exceptions to the orders need be entered. At that point, the computer captures the sales data and retains it for two years, Tourek noted.

The system, which was installed in November 1975, is an IBM 32 with a 16K memory, a 9.1M-byte disk, and a 100 line/min. printer.

The software was developed by Computer Directions, Inc. and was designed for interactive processing, Marilyn Doig of Computer Directions explained.

[July 1977, copyright © *Computerworld*]

# A TEXTILE RENTAL COMPANY

It's sometimes difficult for a small business person operating within the confines of his specialization to find a DP system that fits his needs from among those offered by traditional minicomputer vendors.

So Commercial Towel and Uniform Service, Inc. of Indianapolis, a textile rental firm, took a different approach, according to Theodore Kline, vice-president.

The firm turned to a consultant familiar with both DP and the particular needs of the textile rental industry and then, with several other firms, underwrote the development of a turnkey system designed to fit the textile rental industry's needs.

Each of the firms put up $25,000 to develop the small business system, in a venture that seems to have paid off well for the companies involved.

The mini was just recently installed, Kline noted, and is currently running only the route accounting and accounts receivable application. Future applications that should be running shortly include management information and payroll, Kline added.

Like many small businesses, Commercial began automating its office with the installation of tabulating equipment some 15 years ago. Like others, the firm outgrew this equipment, so Kline began looking around for an alternative.

Although an industry-specific service bureau does exist, the firm thought it "expensive and not flexible" to take this route and so Commercial decided on an in-house system, he said. But the expense of an in-house system configured exactly to the firm's requirements would have been exorbitant.

Commercial wasn't sure what to do until it turned to Markman and Associates of Bala Cynwyd, Pa., which specializes in DP consulting in the textile rental field. The consultants, Herbert Markman and Edward J. Keegan, had a reputation in the industry, Kline noted.

They suggested pooling resources with four other small firms to come up with a system, Markman explained. It seemed like a good idea, so the five companies got together to determine some general criteria for their system.

First, they wanted a system that would not only be adequate for present needs but would be expandable without reprogramming. The system also had to use state-of-the-art equipment, because none of the textile rental firms wanted to outgrow it too quickly or find it obsoleted as soon as it was installed.

All of the companies wanted the mini to be easily operated by present employees. The selection of a vendor was left up to the consulting firm. "We have no one on our staff who has that kind of expertise," Kline explained.

The consulting firm then began its consideration of minicomputer gear. "We did a survey of vendors," Markman recalled, and the list was narrowed to either Hewlett-Packard or Data General Corp. because, among other reasons, "we wanted a financially sound vendor, someone who could give us a consistent supply."

HP "was not price-competitive at that time," he noted, so the firm chose a DG Nova or Eclipse as the basis of the system that was to be installed in each of the five firms. The consultants "sent us all the information and eliminated" all the vendors who did not qualify, Kline noted.

The installation at Commercial includes a 96K Nova 3 CPU with 92M bytes of disk, a 300 line/min. printer, magnetic tape unit, and three CRTs.

The system handles about 6,000 customers. When completed, it should provide the firm with information about customer history according to route, plant, customer, service detail, and items served, he said.

It will also generate reports such as contract renewal reports, customer analysis reports, general ledger, sales analysis, items served, and a new and lost business report.

It also interfaces to industry packages sponsored by the Linen Supply Association of America. One called Computer Assisted Route Development runs on a Control Data Corp. system at the association and is a system for structuring route and optimizing truck routes to minimize time and mileage. The turnkey system produces a tape that interfaces with this system.

[July 1977, copyright © *Computerworld*]


## A COMMODITIES TRADING CENTER

A minicomputer has taken over many of the trading chores at the commercial egg-trading center for the United

States in Durham, N.H. A custom software system lists bids and offers to buy or sell eggs, matches bids and offers, and handles billing and bookkeeping.

The Egg Clearinghouse, Inc. (ECI) operates from a modest office in this New Hampshire college town. Yet last year alone the eight-man staff traded over 300 million eggs with a value of $17 million.

Each day the clearinghouse handles calls from many of its 270 producers and buyers. Ray Delano, ECI president, wanted a system that would take most of the manual tabulation and calculations out of the egg-trading process.

The ECI system includes a file containing an identifying code for each trader. At the start of trading, a trader phones in, gives his identification, and enters his bid or offer.

The system notes the location of each buyer and seller and figures the freight cost between every possible combination of buyers and sellers. It allows for this freight difference when it tries to match bids and offers and make trades.

If the system finds no trades, the mini lists the next best trade for each of the buyers and sellers. Traders can use this information to make price adjustments.

Data on each trade go into an invoice file. Then the system prints a three-part confirmation that lists the details of the agreement—names of buyer and seller, type and quantity of eggs, shipping route, and delivery date. Finally, the system prints a bill to the buyer and a check for the seller.

A summary of each day's trading is also compiled. Applied Systems Inc., who wrote the software, arranged a telephone link with Pennwire, a commodity trader's wire service.

Every ten minutes, the clearinghouse mini dials into this link and sends a summary, and updated information becomes available to traders all over the country.

The clearinghouse system is built around a Digital Equipment Corp. PDP-8/A minicomputer running under Educomp's ETOS time-sharing operating system. The installation has 32K of core memory and uses two RKO-5 disk drives. A Decwriter and four Decscopes complete the equipment.

Delano felt the move to the system was inevitable. "I knew we couldn't continue to expand," he said.

"When there are many price adjustments to bids and offers being made, it's hard to keep track of which two come together first. We would probably have to start taking a trading recess to work through the information without the computer."

## AN INSURANCE COMPANY

Faced with only moderate sales and an inexperienced staff, an insurance agency in Los Angeles managed to boost sales 60 percent in five years from $11 million to $17 million with help from a minicomputer system.

When Charles Vance became head of one of Pacific Mutual's Los Angeles agencies, seven of his top agents were planning to retire or leave the company. New agents would need extensive training as well as years of experience before they could produce at top level.

In order to keep sales from dropping any lower, Vance began a study to determine how to maintain and increase the agency's sales. He found his answer, he said, with a Wang Laboratories, Inc. WCS-20 system and Wang's Lifeline software, which is used as an in-house policy illustration and letter-writing system.

Computerized policy illustrations are one of an insurance company's most effective tools, according to Vance. Before the Wang system was implemented, however, younger agents were reluctant to use them; time-sharing companies charged up to $8 for each illustration and the agents couldn't afford them, Vance explained.

In addition, the time-sharing services didn't allow any flexibility in designing and modifying the illustrations at a reasonable price, Vance said.

In order to find a substitute for time-sharing, Vance and Craig Freeman of Software Systems, Inc., a member of Wang's National Software Vendor Network, developed what has evolved into Lifeline.

With a few input variables such as policy values, age of prospect, dividend and rider options, Vance and his agents can now produce within minutes any illustration necessary for an effective sales call, he said.

The system provides policy illustrations for ledger statements, three-term insurance schedules, flip-flop proposals and schedules for flexible deposit and split-dollar policies.

The system also automatically compares various policies, including those of competitive carriers, in terms of value, premium outlay, and investment return.

The capability of producing limitless illustrations without a charge for each one has encouraged Vance's agents to prepare a variety of proposals to find the best alternative for each customer, he noted.

The system has given new agents confidence in dealing in a sophisticated marketplace and has provided the more experienced agents with increased time to devote to selling instead of working out the complicated proposals, Vance said.

"In five or ten minutes, we can do what it would take a person five or ten days to do with a calculator and a pencil," he added.

In addition to the illustrations, the system features a letter-writing, editing, and mailing list management program that is used to generate new sales leads, stimulate sales from current policyholders, and even recruit new agents, according to Vance.

The interactive Lifeline couples an automatic user-maintained client file with custom-designed letters and memos, stored on floppy diskettes, to deliver personalized mailings, Vance said.

Lifeline extracts names from the file based on any parameters the user selects then automatically inserts the selected information into a prewritten letter.

The Pacific Mutual agency uses Lifeline on Wang's Model 2281W daisy wheel high-speed printer. Vance originally installed a cassette-based Wang system, but later upgraded to a WCS-20 with 16K CPU and Model 2270-2 floppy diskette for faster response time.

[December 1977, copyright © *Computerworld*]

## WALTER A. LEVY

# A Glossary of Computer Terms

**application package**

A set of programs, usually developed by a computer manufacturer or a computer program supplier, that can respond efficiently to a wide variety of requirements within a basic type of application. For example, a payroll package can efficiently handle many kinds of payrolls for many different kinds of companies.

**application programs**

A class of programs, usually developed by computer users, that provide the usable and recognizable data processing services for which the computer is intended. Application programs depend heavily on the foundation provided by system programs.

**Assembler**

A kind of programming language whose source language statements have a simple one-to-one relationship to the computer object language. All source language statements are translated by an assembler program before the object program is run.

**audit trail**

A form of accounting for and recording of events that occur during the processing of a certain group of data to permit after-the-fact review.

*159*

**BAL**
Basic Assembler Language. The standard IBM System 370 Assembler language. The term is sometimes used generically to refer to any assembler language.

**BASIC**
Beginners' All-Purpose Symbolic Instruction Code. A popular programming language that is easy to learn and use on small computers. Many different versions of BASIC have been developed. The language is widely used in educational applications and is now beginning to be used in business applications. Translation of BASIC statements predominantly relies on interpreters, but compiler versions are now also being offered.

**batch processing**
A method of processing in which the work to be performed is accumulated in batches and then handled on a regular basis. For example, if all employee time sheets were to be collected daily and the payroll processed weekly, this would be batch processing. Batch processing methods are widely used because they are reliable, promote good accounting controls and security controls over data processing, and fit easily into the "job shop" method of data center operation.

**bit**
A basic unit of binary information within a computer. A bit is a single digit that may have a value of either 0 or 1 and can therefore represent two possible states of information. Two bits can represent 4 states of information, three bits 8 states, four bits 16 states and so forth.

**byte**
A basic unit of data storage composed of 8 bits and commonly used to store a character of information. A byte is capable of storing any one of 256 different kinds of characters.

**card punch**
A device used to punch information stored in the computer on cards and stack the cards into a deck. Card punches may process 50 to 1,000 cards per minute.

**card reader**
A device used to read a stack of punched cards into the computer. Card readers may process from 50 to 1,000 cards per minute.

**cartridge**
See *Tape Reel.*

**cassette**
See *Tape Reel.*

**central processing unit (CPU)**
The unit that controls program execution. Most computers have only one processor, to which this term somewhat redundantly refers. In larger, more complex computer systems with several processors, the CPU controls the overall system.

**character**
A term generally synonymous with *byte* in today's computers. In older computers, a unit of data storage holding a character consisted of 6 bits, not 8, permitting only 64 kinds of characters to be represented.

**character printer**
A medium- or low-speed printer that can place only one character at a time on paper. The device generally operates in conjunction with a keyboard as an electrically controlled typewriter. Character printers today achieve between 10 and 100 characters per second, or roughly 3 to 50 lines per minute.

**chip**
A tiny piece of pure material such as silicon or sapphire on which integrated circuits are built. The chip is typically one-tenth of an inch square and encapsulated in a plastic envelope about the size of a postage stamp for protection. The term may refer to the entire encapsulated circuit or to just the pure material.

**COBOL**
Common Business-Oriented Language. The predominant programming language for business and financial applications. Its source language statements are particularly suitable to the type of data processing required in business applications. They differ significantly from FORTRAN and BASIC. Translation of COBOL statements into object language is via compiler.

**code**
A group of program statements either written by the user or directly contained in the computer. As a verb, to write code.

**compiler**
A program, usually manufacturer-supplied, that translates source language statements into object program statements. Compilers are much more powerful than assemblers or interpreters, producing a much more useful object program code from a few source language statements, with fewer problems remaining to be solved through testing. For most ordinary data processing applications, compilers are the preferred type of language translator.

**computer**
Any general-purpose electronic data processing system. The principal elements are the processor, memory, peripheral-device controller, and peripheral devices.

**core memory**
A kind of main memory using magnetic cores to hold data. For many years it was the principal physical method of storing data, but it has now been largely supplanted in newer-model computers by semiconductor devices.

**CRT/keyboard terminal**
A popular type of terminal that combines operator data entry and display facilities into a work station. The work station often includes a printer for obtaining a permanent record of the information shown on the video display.

**CRT terminal**
See *video display unit.*

**custom programming**
The act of writing an application program to conform exactly to the specifications of a system without using any previously developed application program.

**data base**
A group of different files serving a broad purpose—for example, the accounting system data base of a company. Also see *data base system.*

**data base system**
A data management system that controls the processing of a large group of files (usually with complex interrelationships) to improve flexibility and efficient use of the data contained in the files. Data base systems are implemented through large and complex system programs.

**data center**
A department of a company responsible for managing one or more computer systems and performing all the services directly related to the use of the computer and the processing of data.

**data management system**
See *file management system.*

**debugging**
Trade jargon for the process of testing and correcting a program.

**decimal digit**
A basic unit of data storage composed of 4 bits and able to store a single decimal digit from 0 to 9. In common practice, two decimal digits are "packed" into a single 8-bit byte for efficiency.

**dedicated computer**
A computer or data center dedicated to a single application and perhaps directly controlled by the user rather than by EDP personnel. If the application is large enough, use of a dedicated computer is a good method of operation. For other applications a job shop approach or time sharing may be more economical.

**disk drive**
The mechanism that holds the rotating disk storage unit, analogous to a phonograph turntable. The term may also refer collectively to the mechanism and the rotating disk storage unit.

**disk file**
The most important type of file storage unit in use today. The unit consists of a rotating disk on which information is recorded magnetically. Data are written to or read from the disk by means of a magnetic head that is positioned on various tracks on the disk. The term also refers to a file of data stored on a portion of a rotating disk or on several such disks.

**disk pack (disk cartridge)**
A data storage unit that can be removed from the disk drive mechanism and replaced with another. It is analogous to a phonograph record, with the disk drive the equivalent of a turntable.

**diskette**
Trade name for a small floppy disk.

**display**

The portion of a terminal where an operator can see information provided by the computer. The most commonly used display is a cathode ray tube (CRT).

**DP**

Common abbreviation for data processing.

**EDP**

Common abbreviation for electronic data processing.

**erasable/programmable read-only memory (EPROM)**

A read-only memory whose contents cannot be altered by normal computer operation but can be changed by a special procedure using auxiliary equipment.

**field**

A piece of data contained within a record, consisting of one or more characters and having a single integrated meaning. For example, an accounts receivable record may have a name-address field.

**file**

A group of related records identical in format that are collected and often processed together. For example, a file may contain all the accounts receivable records of the company or all the accounts receivable records showing past-due balances.

**file management system**

A set of system programs used to control the storage and manipulation of files of data. File management systems are quite flexible and can be used efficiently by most application programs.

**file storage unit**

Any peripheral device designed to hold files of data and programs and to make them accessible to the central processor within seconds. Devices of this type are also referred to as mass-memory devices.

**firmware**

Trade jargon for programs stored in a read-only memory whose contents usually are not accessible to normal program operation. Firmware generally performs underlying functions in the computer system such as emulation of an old computer on a new one.

**floppy disk**

An inexpensive type of disk file mechanism commonly used in microcomputers and intelligent terminals. The disk cartridge is a flexible disk similar to but softer and smaller than an LP record.

**FORTRAN**
Formula Translator. The predominant programming language used in scientific and engineering applications. FORTRAN statements are similar to those of BASIC. A compiler is used to translate FORTRAN source statements into object statements.

**hardware**
Trade jargon for the physical equipment of the computer.

**hexadecimal digit**
A basic unit of data storage, composed of 4 bits and used to represent the ten decimal digit values 0–9 plus 6 additional values, commonly labeled A through F. A hexadecimal digit is the same size as a decimal digit but differs in that the full 16 possible states of the 4 bits are used.

**input-output device**
Any peripheral device that permits data to be entered into or obtained from the computer. The term can also refer to file storage devices.

**integrated circuit**
The basic physical building block of modern computers, a single electronic device with dozens to thousands of basic electronic elements fabricated on a thin semiconductor "chip." Integrated circuits are extremely small, inexpensive, and very powerful computationally.

**intelligent terminal**
A terminal with operator data entry and display facilities plus its own processor, main memory, and (perhaps) mass memory. Such a terminal is capable of performing modest data processing functions independently of the computer it services; hence the term "intelligent."

**interpreter**
A computer program, usually manufacturer-supplied, that translates one source statement at a time into computer object code, lets the computer execute the object code statement, then returns to the source language program for the next statement. Interpreters are suitable only for low-volume, relatively simple programs.

**interrogate**
See *query*.

**item**
A single piece of data (or field) or a collection of data consisting of several fields. For example, a program may define customer name as one field, address as a second field, and the two fields collectively as the name-address item.

**job shop**
A mode of data center operation in which the data center management schedules and carries out the work requested by users. Job shops can handle many applications at very low cost through efficient use of the computer.

**K**
A multiplier suffix denoting a factor of 1024. For example, *2K bytes* means 2048 bytes. The term may be used by itself, as in "2K," where the implied true meaning is clear.

**keyboard**
The portion of a terminal where the operator enters information.

**keyboard printer/terminal**
A popular terminal that consists of a typewriter device with computer access privileges.

**kilobyte**
A unit of 1,024 bytes; commonly approximated as 1,000 bytes.

**language translator**
A system program that translates the programs written in a particular source language into an object program for use by the computer. In speaking of a language, manufacturers and others in the data processing field sometimes ambiguously refer both to the language itself and to the translator program for that language.

**large-scale integration (LSI)**
Integrated circuits holding hundreds to thousands of basic electronic elements.

**line printer**
A high-speed printer able to print many characters of a single line of print simultaneously. Speeds typically range from 300 to 2,000 (132-character) lines per minute.

**local terminal**
A terminal within the same room or building as the computer it services.

## M
A multiplier prefix denoting a factor of 1,048,576, or 1,024 multiplied by 1,024. Synonymous with *Meg* or *Mega*.

### main memory
The memory module directly used by the processor to obtain programs and data. It may be constructed of magnetic core material or semiconductor devices. It has no moving parts and allows the processor to obtain access to any byte of data in less than two-millionths of a second.

### management information system (MIS)
A broad term loosely referring to a set of files and programs that assist business managers in dealing with the nonroutine decision-making aspects of their jobs.

### mass memory
A device other than main memory that can store large files of data at much lower cost per unit of storage capacity than main memory. Mass-memory devices are generally electromechanical, with moving parts, and are much slower than main memory.

### medium-scale integration (MSI)
Integrated circuits holding dozens to hundreds of electronic elements.

### megabyte
A unit of 1,048,576 bytes, or 1,024 kilobytes; commonly approximated as 1,000,000 bytes.

### memory
A device into which data and programs can be entered for storage and from which they can be retrieved as needed. Used alone, "memory" generally signifies the main memory of the computer.

### Memory address
A specific location within a memory device at which data may be found. The term also refers to the information provided to the memory device itself so as to identify that location.

### microcomputer
A computer composed of a microprocessor, semiconductor memory, and simple peripheral devices. Today's microcomputers are marketed for very small and simple applications, such as video games, automobile ignition control, and scientific instruments.

**microprocessor**
A complete central processor containing tens of thousands of basic electronic elements and built of between one and three large-scale integration (LSI) devices. In a microcomputer, the microprocessor is about the same size as a deck of playing cards.

**microsecond**
One-millionth of a second. Modern computers generally execute each instruction in less than 5 microseconds. Modern main memories generally provide data to the processor in less than one microsecond.

**millisecond**
One-thousandth of a second. Modern computer mass-memory devices generally respond to program requests for data in several dozen milliseconds.

**minicomputer**
A small, relatively inexpensive computer composed of a central processor, at least one input-output device, and primary storage capacity of up to 64K bytes. Today differences between computers are sometimes due more to historical and marketing factors than to technical factors.

**modularity**
The property of a computer system composed of modules. A system with a high degree of modularity can be easily adapted to a wide variety of purposes.

**module**
A piece of electronic equipment or unit of a program or data file that has a unique purpose and that can be connected to similar modules in building-block fashion to create a larger, more complex structure. Computer technology, both hardware and software, depends heavily on the concept of the module.

**object language**
A language whose statements were produced by a language translator from source language statements. Computer programs may go through several such translations, where the object language statements produced by one translator become the source language statements for the next. The final object language form, called *machine language,* is the form that the computer actually uses.

## off-line processing
Data processing functions that can be performed on a regular, scheduled basis. For example, a credit authorization service must be on line, but customer account processing can be performed off line in a batch mode.

## on-line processing
A method of data processing in which work is presented to the computer in single transactions at the convenience of the user; the computer responds quickly, often within seconds. For example, with an on-line credit authorization service a clerk at the cash register can verify a customer's account immediately before approving a credit sale. On-line processing methods are much more expensive than batch processing methods, but they provide an essential service for certain applications.

## operating system
A central system program that manages all other programs on a computer. Few computers today are run without an operating system.

## override feature
A procedure for bypassing restrictive or protective parts of a computer program in order to deal with special problems.

## package installation
The process of selecting the options and controls for a general-purpose application package so that it will meet a particular user's requirements, physically installing the package on the user's computer, and training personnel. Installation is generally performed by the company that sells the package.

## password
A security procedure for preventing unauthorized access to files that contain confidential or valuable data. The password generally entails a control procedure in which a user signs on to the system at a terminal and makes a request for access to a file. The procedure is particularly important in on-line systems, where there is considerably greater risk of unauthorized access than in batch processing systems.

## peripheral device
A device, physically separate from the processor and its main memory, that is used to store large files of data or to permit data to be

entered into or obtained from the computer. Peripheral devices used to store large files of data are generally called *file storage units;* those used to enter or receive data from the computer are known as *input-output devices.*

**peripheral device controller**
A specialized processor that connects the peripheral devices to the processor of the computer and its main memory.

**PL/I**
Programming Language I. A new type of programming language that combines features of both COBOL and FORTRAN. It is not yet as widely used. PL/I is a prototype of PL/M and PL/Z, similar languages that are now being used on microcomputers. As for FORTRAN and COBOL, translation into object language is via compiler.

**port**
An electrical path providing peripheral devices access to the central processor of the computer, usually through a peripheral device controller.

**printer**
A device that prints out information in the computer in readable form on paper. Printers are rated in either characters per second or lines per minute (a line is usually 132 characters wide). They vary as to the size of paper and the availability of special forms-handling features.

**processor**
The "intelligent" element of a computer system that executes the programs stored in its memory. Processors today routinely execute hundreds of thousands of program steps per second.

**program**
A set of instructions directing a computer to process data in a specific manner. The program is written in a language convenient for the user, translated into a form acceptable for the computer, and sorted in its memory. The processor of the computer executes the program.

**query**
The process by which a user obtains information from a computer by making an inquiry at a terminal.

### random-access memory (RAM)
A memory device in which data can be obtained with equal convenience and speed from any location. Compare *sequential-access memory*.

### read-only memory (ROM)
A memory device whose contents have been fixed during manufacture so that they can be read, but not changed, by the computer. This type of device is often used to store simple programs where the reliability of the system is important or where it is very difficult to reload programs.

### read/write memory (RWM)
A memory device allowing programs to read or write data into any location. The act of writing data into a memory location destroys the previous contents at that location. In microcomputer literature, frequently abbreviated *RAM*.

### real-time processing
The processing and recording of data at the moment the related physical transaction occurs. Synonymous with *on-line processing*, although some writers mistakenly try to draw a distinction between the two terms.

### record
Broadly, a unit of data storage in which several distinct pieces of information are collected for an organized purpose. For example, an accounts receivable record may contain all the facts about a particular customer.

### remote terminal
A terminal that is some distance away from the computer it services, often connected by telephone lines.

### semiconductor memory
A type of main memory that uses integrated circuits, or semiconductor devices, to hold data. This is the only form of main memory in microcomputers.

### sequential-access memory
A memory device, such as a magnetic tape, necessitating a serial search to enter or retrieve data. For such memories, the time required to obtain a desired piece of information depends on its exact location. Compare *random-access memory*.

**service bureau**

A data center that performs services for its customers, charging a price based on costs and market factors.

**software**

Trade jargon for the programs used to run the computer system. The term is sometimes also used to describe documentation of the programs or the operating procedures of the system as well as the programs themselves.

**source language**

A language used to write computer programs. The source language must be translated into an object language before it can be used by the computer.

**specification**

A document that precisely and thoroughly describes a system or program.

**subroutine**

A small program module that can be used repetitively as a building block for many different types of programs.

**system analysis**

The process of studying business problems and expressing them in systematic terms before designing a computer system to solve the problems. The term is greatly misused to describe *system design,* which is a separate process.

**system design**

The process of designing a solution to a business problem in computer terms sufficiently complete so that the solution may be implemented by programs, without further study of the business aspects of the problem.

**system programs**

A class of programs, usually furnished by the manufacturer of the computer, that reduces the work required by computer users to obtain the data processing services they want. System programs provide a foundation for application programs but in themselves do not produce visible end results. The most common system programs in use today are operating systems, language translators, and file management systems.

**tape file**
A file of data stored on magnetic tape. The storage device itself may be a reel of tape, a cartridge, or a cassette; all these devices are separate from the tape drive mechanism itself. Access to information stored in the file requires searching the length of the tape until the information is found. It may take several minutes.

**tape reel, cassette, cartridge**
Physical devices on which magnetic tape files are stored.

**tape station or drive**
The mechanism on which tape reels or cassettes are placed.

**temperate room**
Referring to the air conditioning needs of a computer, this term implies that no measures are required beyond those provided for the ordinary comfort of personnel.

**terminal**
Any device allowing an operator to enter a request for information from a computer. In most cases the terminal is some distance from the computer to which it is connected.

**time sharing**
A method of letting many users share access to a large computer, each user operating on line as though no one else were using the computer. In time-sharing systems each user may manage his own programs and data without reference to what the other users are doing. The economic penalty for computer sharing is occasional delay and the need for a rather large computer. Time sharing is very important in program development and experimental applications. It is not important in production data processing.

**turnkey**
A method of doing business in which a vendor takes full responsibility for developing and installing a data processing system. The turnkey approach generally involves a contractual commitment between vendor and user and is often used by businesses that do not have the personnel to develop the required data processing system.

**video display unit (VDU)**
A terminal that uses a cathode ray tube (CRT) display.

# Index